DECORATIVE
painting

Maria Victoria Lopez Santacruz

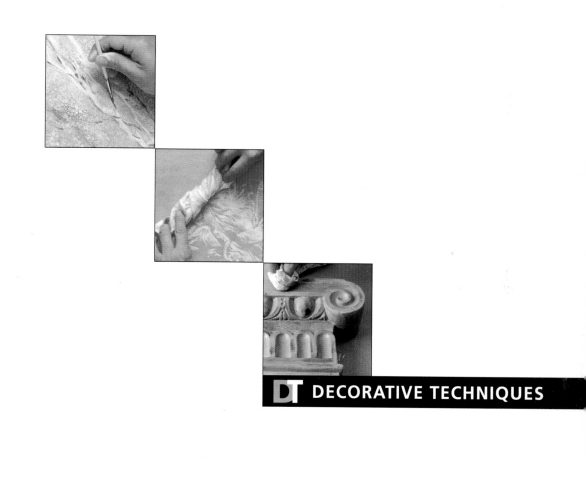

DT DECORATIVE TECHNIQUES

BARRON'S

DECORATIVE
painting

BARRON'S

Contents

chapter

WATER TECHNIQUES

DECORATING WITH WATER TECHNIQUES

chapter

OIL TECHNIQUES

DECORATING WITH OIL TECHNIQUES

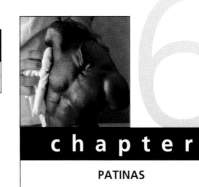

chapter

PATINAS

DECORATING WITH PATINAS

Introduction

finishes and textures created with decorative painting can transform any space into a more attractive and pleasant environment. The purpose of decorating is to personalize furniture, objects, and walls. Decorative painting knows no bounds; techniques and creativity produce unexpected finishes, tying together everything around us and uniting color, texture, and special effects. The information in this book can be used by beginning painters as well as professionals who have plenty of experience. This is a practical guide that presents many finishes that can be improved or modified, depending on who uses them and where they are applied.

The first chapters deal with the origins of decorative painting and its applications. After that, you'll find lots of information about brushes, tools, and materials commonly used in creating different decorative effects. Starting with chapter 4 there are step-by-step instructions and photos covering different techniques and materials for various finishes created through proper preparation and decorative painting on various surfaces such as wood, plaster, walls, and others. The many techniques presented in this book will help you create attractive decors and striking effects on any number of objects. You will also find instructions on how to make paints from natural pigments and other basic ingredients.

Maria Victoria Lopez Santacruz

Decorative painting: origins and materials

Decorative painting is one of the most important pillars of the decorating world because of its adaptability to every style and practically every material. It's a way of modifying and beautifying our surroundings. Throughout the history of decoration and in all civilizations, countless effects have been created that have ennobled and expressed a personality or a style passed down through the centuries. People have always been deeply interested in using their innate creativity in adorning their surroundings, especially by adding decoration to walls and objects that are lacking in beauty. Decorative painting allows people to add a personal touch to their surroundings, can be adapted to all styles and shapes, and provides options appropriate to every skill level.

What is decorative painting?

For centuries decorators have used decorative painting as a means to beautify objects and rooms, facades and interiors of buildings, and to imitate different materials that usually are very costly, such as marble, woods, and precious stones, in order to create a striking visual effect. Decorative painting enables us to give a personal touch to walls and furniture, and to create effects and finishes that beautify our surroundings.

Origins and historical information

Remnants of decorative painting have been found in practically all ancient cultures. Even before recorded history, people were decorating cave walls with hunting scenes as a symbolic ritual and a means of artistic expression.

Many ancient civilizations such as Egypt, Greece, and Rome also used paint to decorated the interiors and exteriors of temples, houses, and buildings. This necessary artistic expression is most refined in Pompeii, where beautiful decorations with ornamental, painted details are still preserved for our enjoyment. An example is the house of Livia, where some beautifully decorated walls still exist.

If we examine the various applications of paint in the past, we can see that there once existed a profession that nowadays is undergoing a revival: that of the decorative painter.

In many cultures, such as in Africa and Central America, pigments and paints were considered sacred gifts from the earth. They were also used in rituals to decorate the human body, clothing, and houses.

Creativity in the visual arts is found in practically all ages, from prehistoric painted vases and medieval frescos to the innovative designs of the German Bauhaus school, which marked a revolution in the contemporary world of decoration before the Second World War.

At some points in history, especially in

the Renaissance toward the end of the fifteenth century and the start of the sixteenth, painting was practically a privilege in the service of religion, since social changes, wars, and geographical displacements left no room for it at other levels of society. That's why many times great sculptural treasures are found in churches and cathedrals; religious themes predominated, since the arts were patronized by the economic power of the church.

Throughout the centuries a countless number of finishes and effects created in paint have been used to decorate all kinds of furniture, objects, and walls as an alternative to a plain, smooth finish.

Starting in the seventeenth century, it became fashionable to surround oneself with such materials as exotic woods, tortoiseshell, precious stones, brocade, and the magnificence of gold. All that was achieved by means of lower-cost painted imitations.

Creativity is what impels people to search for and experiment with new textures and reproduce different materials.

A marvelous fresco at an eighteenth-century temple, painted over ancient frescos on Sulamini's wall in Bagan, a city in old Burma.

Techniques through the ages

Delving into old manuals on painting techniques reveals some strange formulas that painters used in the olden days to make paints by preparing glues mixed with earth and pigments. They boiled sheep or rabbit skins and some animal bones until they became gelatinous, and then mixed them with liquids and dissolved pigments in them. Whey obtained from milk or cheese was also used as an agglutinating agent or binder in painting murals, walls, and furniture. Nowadays an equivalent known as casein is used in craft painting. This type of paint is also used in the simple and pleasing Shaker style. Plant and tree resins have been used in formulas throughout the ages to create paints. Many of these formulas, some of which are very curious and original, are still used in craft painting.

Cheerful colors applied tastefully can be used to decorate the facades of buildings. An example of this is the intense pink used on this house, which is located in the Triana neighborhood of Seville, Spain.

Trends

The trend in contemporary painting is a rediscovery of traditional finishes and paints, using softer colors to create effects and environments of past ages. An example of this is the Arts and Crafts movement, which finds its inspiration in the Middle Ages, using four hundred years later practically the same palette of colors made with natural pigments: earthy colors, dark reds, ochres, browns, greens, and blues.

We're fortunate to be able to obtain materials identical or comparable to ones that were used years ago, such as special brushes that are now mass-produced. This enables us to imitate the old techniques with practically the same tools and products that were used long ago, but with the advantage of a broad range of products of modern manufacture.

Historical references can lead us to materials and color choices based on certain styles and information appropriate to different countries or geographical areas. All this can help us in reproducing environments created by means of texture and color. Gray-greens make us think of Scandinavia; saffrons, reds, and purples transport us to Central America; and luminous pastel tones suggest Cuba. Sparkling blues, warm reds, red ochres, and soft pinks remind us of the Mediterranean sun, and siennas and terra-cottas evoke France and Italy.

Trends continually change, so it's important to do the necessary research before trying to create special effects based on time period or style.

Application

The application of decorative painting has practically no limits, since it can be adapted perfectly to any kind of surface. The main thing is the creativity of the person who's doing it. Small objects, furniture, and walls can be decorated with a countless number of decorative effects from the simplest to the most elaborate.

Surface preparation is the key to achieving good results. Given adequate preparation of the substrate—whether fragile or strong, porous or plastic—a decorative finish can be applied to any surface. That allows us to personalize any space or object. It's important to keep in mind, especially in decorating living areas, that you have to deal with a broad spectrum of factors such as space, proportion, illumination, and texture.

Sometimes painting is used not only as a decorative element, but also as a way to mask underlying problems and defects.

Polychrome chair combining carved relief decoration and silver leaf, with egg tempera red paint.

Materials

There's a great variety of materials that are used to create perfect finishes. Inadequate tools can often spoil the desired results; proper use of the right equipment enables us to create very simple effects and a high-quality finish. In specialty stores you can find selections of materials and tools needed for applying decorative techniques. This section will show you some of the tools most commonly used in decorative painting. You won't need to use all of them, but it's at least useful to know about them.

Different types of brushes

There are many types of brushes that can be used for different types of work. A few of them are used only to create very specific effects. The quality of each brush depends on the type of bristle and the kind of handle that it's made with; the brush is made up of the bristles and the handle, which often are joined by a metal ferrule. There's also a wide variety of sizes that are used according to the size of the surface to be decorated.

Brushes

• Boar's bristle brushes
Bristle brushes are the most versatile ones, and they hold a lot of paint; this makes them perfect for covering large areas. You can buy brushes with almond-shaped points that are used for more delicate work, reaching into corners, and working paint into moldings.

• Old-world brushes
These brushes are used for oil paints and varnishes. They come in different shapes and sizes. The bristles are black boar, and since they are fairly soft they don't leave brush marks.

• Horsehair brushes
These brushes are made from long horse-hair; they are used to create imitation wood grain. When used for striking, pressing, or dragging across the surface, they create different effects; they can also be used to imitate the texture of fabric.

Old-world brushes.

Bristle brushes.

Horsehair brushes.

Rounded natural bristle pencil brushes.

Flat natural bristle brushes.

Squirrel-hair brush.

Pencil brushes

• Rounded natural bristle brushes

Usually these bristle brushes are very economical and useful for painting and mixing. They can also be used to apply different materials such as wax, talc, asphaltum, and others.

• Flat natural bristle brushes

These brushes are used for oil and water paints; since they are flat, they hold less paint.

• Artists' brushes

These can be made of natural or synthetic bristles; the latter are cheaper. They come in a wide variety of shapes and sizes; round ones are used more for watercolors, and flat ones for oils. They are used for the most delicate freehand work.

Graining brushes

These brushes are very useful in creating marblelike streaks. They come in different lengths and thicknesses of bristle and are made of soft natural bristles.

Angle brushes

Made of natural bristle, they come in different widths and are used to paint lines and edging. They are best suited for use with oils.

Lining brushes

These are also known as feather brushes. They are used to paint lines on furniture and walls. They are made with hairs from a calf's ear. Since they hold a lot of paint, they can be used for long strokes.

• Squirrel-hair brush

As the name indicates, this brush is made from squirrel hair. It's used to imitate the streaks in marble and to create some imitation wood grains. It's suitable for use only with oil paints.

• Stenciling brushes

Stenciling brushes come in several sizes and qualities, and are made of natural and artificial bristles. Their flat ends make them ideal for painting stencils. Their short, bushy bristles make it easier to control the amount of paint applied. They are held perpendicular to the surface.

Artists' brushes.

Woodgraining brushes.

Angle brushes.

Stenciling brushes.

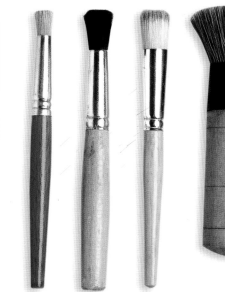

Lining brushes.

China bristle or chip brushes.

Natural-bristle sash brushes.

Synthetic-bristle sash brushes.

Finishing brush.

Sash Brushes

• Natural-bristle sash brushes

There are different types sash brushes made with boar's bristles; they are useful for oil- and water-based paints and for any small-scale work. Normally they are used for painting window sashes.

• Synthetic-bristle sash brushes

Essentially these are used for water-based finishes; their soft, synthetic bristles create a uniform and smooth finish. They are easy to clean and take care of.

• Finishing brush

This is used for delicate work with varnish and lacquer. This type of brush is made from very soft squirrel hair.

• Broad brushes

These are made with short natural bristles. They are suited to covering large areas. When used dry, they drag and distribute paint to create different effects. They are flexible and can be used to cover large areas.

• Woodgraining brushes

These are made with natural bristles of varying lengths. They're well suited to use with oil-based paints; when dragged perpendicular to the surface, they create a graining effect. There are also other types—pipe overgrainers—where the bristles are clustered into small bunches like pencil brushes; these are available in different widths. This type of brush marks lightly and mimics wood grain. It is also used to add broader stripes to the work.

Stippling brush.

Other Types of Brushes

• China bristle or chip brushes

These are like natural bristle sash brushes, but with shorter bristles. They are used to distribute and spread out glazes and to create dragging or striping effects.

• Natural bristle fan brush

This is used for oil paints to create broad brush strokes using only a little paint; it can also be used to create wood grain by dragging. Fan brushes made of squirrel hair are intended for use with water paints.

• Stippling brushes

These brushes are made with natural bristles and come in different sizes. They are used for decorative finishes such as stippling with oil paints.

• Smoothers and blenders

These brushes have become very popular in decorative painting. The best ones are made of badger hair, and their price varies according to the size of the brush and the quality of the hair. Only the tip of the bristles is used to brush the surface lightly and create a perfect finish. This brush simultaneously smoothes and integrates different layers of glaze.

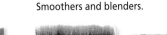

Bristle fan blender.

Broad brushes.

Woodgraining brushes.

Smoothers and blenders.

Applicators

In addition to the many types of brushes that are available in the marketplace, there are some other tools that make it easier and more enjoyable to apply paint. These are used mainly to paint surfaces that later will be given special treatment and to create special effects. The different types of foam, wool, and plush rollers are great for applying uniform coats to large and medium-size areas. Good results always depend on proper preparation for the base coats. In addition, rags, sponges, and small foam-rubber applicators shaped like brushes are used to apply paints, primers, and varnishes. Sponges, rags, and spatulas are also sometimes used to apply paint or to create textures and different effects.

Rollers

Rollers are very useful for spreading base coats evenly and for covering large areas. They are made in various sizes and textures. The nap of the roller determines its suitability for oil or water paints. Rollers are also used for applying varnish over large areas; they speed up the job and make for a uniform finish.

Synthetic sponges

Synthetic sponges are more economical to use than natural sponges; they are used to create various decorative effects. They are available in various shapes, sizes, and textures.

Cotton rags

This type of rag is used both for cleaning tools and for creating various decorative effects. Cotton rags are recommended because they are the most absorbent.

• Scrub brushes made from plant fibers

Brushes made from plant fibers are used to smooth out large and small surfaces and give them an aged appearance. They

are less abrasive than common sand-papers.

A plant-fiber scrub brush is ideal for whitewash because it covers large areas. Before using the brush, it's a good idea to soften it by soaking.

• Foam applicators

These applicators are relatively new to the market. They are used to paint smooth surfaces; they produce a uniform, smooth finish without leaving brush marks. They are appropriate for small or medium areas. They are made of foam rubber and can be used with water and oil paints, but not with gum lacquer.

• Rubber combs and pads

These are used to create various effects, from imitation wood grain to fantasy finishes. They come in different widths and shapes and may be made of hard or soft rubber. You can use them to create all kinds of decorative effects with oil paints when you drag them across a painted surface.

• Natural sponges

Although they're more expensive than synthetic sponges, these sponges are the best for creating decorative effects. They come in different sizes and textures.

Foam applicators.

Rubber combs and pads.

Rollers.

Natural sponges.

Synthetic sponges.

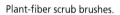
Plant-fiber scrub brushes.

Other tools

In addition to brushes, many other tools are often needed to help in the decorative process, and they assure satisfactory results. Many of them are easy to find, and some are already present in our homes. Not all of them will be needed for every job; they are used according to the intended finish and the project.

• Level
Levels are indispensable for marking straight lines on walls and leveling all types of horizontal decorations with respect to the floor and the ceiling of a room.

• Burlap
Different materials besides brushes are often used to create decorative effects. Burlap is used to simulate wood grain and to impress its weave on the surface being worked.

• Scrapers
These are very useful for mixing and applying spackling compound and plaster, and for scraping dried coats of paint. They come in different widths. Square scrapers used for auto body work are useful in texturing different types of surfaces.

• Latex gloves
Disposable gloves protect the skin from materials that are hard to wash off, or even toxic. These should be used whenever you work with such materials.

• Adhesive or masking tape
Tape is used to secure stencils and protect areas you don't want to paint. Be careful when creating stripes or lines with tape so that the paint doesn't get underneath it. It's not a good idea to leave tape in place for longer than 24 hours.

• Plumb line
This is one of the most important tools in decorating. It's used to mark off lines on large surfaces and, in conjunction with the level, to be sure that lines on walls are straight.

• Chamois cloths
These are very useful for applying waxes and polishing finishes, and for removing dust.

Plastic sheeting.

Adhesive and masking tapes.

Plumb line.

Chamois cloths

Putty knives.

Level.

Burlap.

Latex gloves.

Scrapers.

• Plastic sheeting

This is essential for protecting floors and furniture in rooms that are to be painted. It's also useful in creating different decorative effects with glazes.

• Sandpaper

This is indispensable in achieving a good finish and preparing the surface to be decorated. Sometimes sandpaper is used to create an appearance of wear. There is a wide selection of sandpapers in grits varying from coarse to extra-fine. You can also get wet-or-dry sand-paper that is used moistened with water to produce very smooth finishes.

• Steel wool

Steel wool can be had in various grades from very coarse and abrasive to very fine for smooth finishes. It is used much like sandpaper, and can be used to abrade or to polish, depending on the grade.

• Containers

It's important to keep on hand different types of containers for mixing paints and other preparations. You'll need small containers such as tin cans and some larger plastic ones. The size you choose will depend on the size of the area you have to cover.

• Wire brush

A wire brush is used to scrape and remove rust from metals; it's also used to abrade. It can lend an appearance of age to the finish on various pieces.

• Measuring tape

A stiff metal measuring tape is used to measure areas of all sizes. Measuring tapes are available in various lengths. They're particularly useful in taking vertical measurements.

• Knives and scissors

Scalpels, hobbyists' knives, and scissors are used mainly for cutting strips and templates for stenciling; several models are available, including ones that pivot for cutting curves.

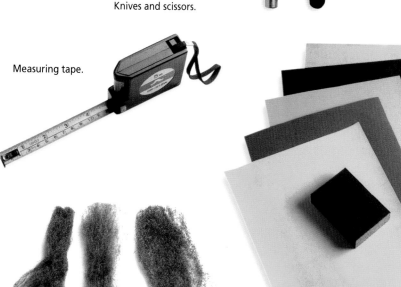

Knives and scissors.

Measuring tape.

Sandpaper.

Steel wool.

Wire brush.

Containers.

Cleaning and maintenance

Keeping brushes, applicators, and other materials used for different finishes and effects in good condition is mostly a function of keeping them clean. Some brushes and applicators are very inexpensive, but that doesn't mean they shouldn't be kept clean. Others are much more costly, and they surely need to be treated with the greatest of care so that they'll last as long as possible. So even though this process may be tedious, it's essential, since oftentimes, well-used brushes produce better results than new ones, which may shed hairs and leave dust.

New brushes and sponges

New brushes must be washed very thoroughly with hot water before using them to remove the dust that they may pick up in storage and to eliminate the loose bristles that are common to new brushes. Washings are repeated until the brushes cease to lose bristles. This step is especially important in preparing brushes for use with varnish. Hold the brushes by the handle between both hands and spin them energetically; this also gets rid of loose hairs.

New natural sponges should be soaked several times in warm water to eliminate sand and dried algae.

If you have to interrupt your work, it's important to keep the brushes and applicators from drying out.

When working with alkyd paints, submerge the brushes and rollers in water and shake them out well when you resume work. If you're using vinyl or acrylic paint, wrap the brushes in plastic to keep the paint from drying.

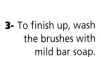

1- Get rid of excess alkyd or oil paint by dabbing on newspaper.

2- If the brushes don't have too much paint on them, they can be put into a container with turpentine and spun vigorously until they are clean.

3- To finish up, wash the brushes with mild bar soap.

Brushes used with alkyd or oil-based paints

Alkyd or oil paints are removed from brushes and rollers by first wiping off as much paint as possible with newspaper. Then they are placed into a container with turpentine and swished around until all the paint comes out of the bristles. After that, the brushes are washed with warm water and mild soap; don't use detergents, since they may harm the natural oils in the bristles. Next, rinse the brushes to remove all traces of soap. Finally, shake them forcefully to eliminate most of the water, and smooth the bristles out straight to help them keep their original shape.

• Other tools

Natural and synthetic sponges are usually used with oil-based glazes, which are easier to remove than acrylic ones.

To wash sponges, remove excess glaze with paper, and then soak them in turpentine to remove the rest of the paint; next, wash them with hot water and mild soap, and rinse with water, making sure that all soap is removed. Let them dry thoroughly before putting them away. Rubber combs and pads are cleaned in the same way as natural and synthetic sponges.

4- It's a good idea to hang the brushes like this so that the bristles keep their natural shape.

5- Brushes are kept in a container with the bristles up so that they keep their original shape.

Brushes used with water-based paints

Acrylic or latex paints are very difficult to remove once they have dried, so it's important to clean brushes, rollers, and other equipment as soon as possible.

A spatula and a wire brush used with care are very useful in removing excess paint from coarse bristles.

Rinse brushes with plenty of water until they come out clean, moving them around in a bucket or a bowl so that the water can circulate among the bristles; change the water frequently. Apply mild soap up to the metal ferrule and then rinse them several times to remove the soap. Hang them up to dry the same way as other brushes.

If the paint has dried on the brush, soak it in denatured alcohol and spread the bristles with your fingers to let the alcohol penetrate; after a few minutes, use mild soap and plenty of water to clean the bristles. Some natural-bristle brushes are very delicate—for example, ones used for marbling and ones made from squirrel hair that are used only for techniques in oil. These are cleaned in turpentine and then impregnated with Vaseline to preserve their shape and quality. Before using them again, the Vaseline is removed with turpentine.

Natural- or synthetic-bristle artists' brushes must be washed with great care, the same way as other brushes and rollers, and in accordance with the technique used. The main thing is that they keep their shape; don't leave them standing on their bristles in a container. They have to be treated with the greatest of care so they remain like new. Artists' brushes usually have a little plastic sleeve to help preserve the shape of the bristles.

1- It's important to rinse brushes in plenty of water.

2- Use a brush to remove excess paint.

3- To preserve natural-bristle brushes, it's a good idea to impregnate them with Vaseline; this helps them keep their form and keeps the bristles in good condition.

• Other tools

All materials, including natural and synthetic sponges, that are used with water-based paints are rinsed well in warm water to remove all traces of paint; then they are washed with mild soap and rinsed with lots of water until all the soap is gone.

Caution

It's essential that rags and pieces of cotton cloth used to create effects with oil glazes or varnishes be allowed to dry in the air; they should never be left moist or piled up. If they must be thrown away, they should be wet with water; since they are very flammable, there is a danger of spontaneous combustion.

Storage

Some natural-bristle brushes, such as those made of badger, should be wrapped in cardboard held in place with adhesive tape or a rubber band; this keeps the bristles from spreading and helps maintain the original shape.

If the equipment is not going to be used for a while, it's best to clean it well and store it in a drawer or a box once it's dry; that keeps it from picking up dust and helps retain its shape.

Natural-bristle brushes should be wrapped in cardboard held in place with adhesive tape or a rubber band to preserve the original shape.

2 Color

Color
is undoubtedly the first thing that
people perceive in their surroundings. The
whole world is a great palette of colors, shades, and
tones that are accessible to us in such a way that, as we
observe nature and our daily surroundings, they provide us with
an endless source of inspiration.

In the combinations that are used to define decorative styles, color is
the basis that unifies and creates environments that are marked with a
personal touch. Even though at certain times in history some colors
were very difficult to obtain, there is no doubt that they made history,
evolving with time, changing according to current tastes, and im-
proving the quality of life of the people who used them to decorate
their surroundings.

As a form of expression, color communicates many
sensations; it also transforms everything around
us and gives it life.

Color as a source of inspiration

There are color cards that show an endless variety of hues from pastels to bright colors, including shades of the primary colors. Colors define different historical periods that can be a source of inspiration. Earthy colors and intense reds, blues, and greens are typical of the Middle Ages. In the decade of 1920 to 1930, Art Deco made white and beige backgrounds fashionable and inspired color combinations involving subdued shades.

Nowadays people are opting for colors almost intuitively, using brighter shades and more elaborate finishes.

Color in the world

When travelers visit other countries, what usually sticks in their mind is the colors that prevail in certain places, their intensity, and their combinations.

In all places throughout the world the inhabitants usually use the colors of the earth in their region because they are easy and economical to obtain. Some colors are known by the name of the region they come from, such as English red, India red, and sienna. All of these are variations of red oxides or ochre earth.

We identify the charm of colors and their diversity according to the country and even the climate where they are used. Light blue, gray, ochre, and red barns transport us to New England. Bold, vibrant, and electric combinations of red, magenta, bright yellows, and brilliant blues and greens may remind us of Mexico and sunny tropical countries.

In Belgium, Holland, and Germany a very characteristic dark green is used to paint doors and windows. A soft, serene green with blue overtones that's almost gray is characteristic of Scandinavia;

other countries have been inspired by it, especially in decorating furniture. Warm reds and earthy ochres are associated with Italy, which likewise is a source of inspiration. In Spain, Portugal, and Greece, luminous whitewash, often combined with different shades of blue, makes us think of the Mediterranean.

Warm colors, natural sienna and ochre, combine nicely on the facades of these houses on the main square of Cuenca, Spain.

Color is present everywhere as an element that beautifies our surroundings. Here is a sample of roofs in cheerful colors from the city of Reykjavik, Iceland.

Color in nature

Nature is a source of inspiration for color; some colors get their name from it, such as lemon yellow, leaf green, chestnut, night blue, and sky blue. Nature contributes immensely to the inexhaustible vocabulary of colors.

In addition, nature not only gives rise to ideas about color, but it also supplies colors and hues in the form of natural pigments and dyes. The most ancient colors are derived from the earth, such as ochre and the siennas that come from clays. Some colors come from plants and insects, such as the vegetable indigo that comes from the leaves of a plant indigenous to India, and purple, which is derived from the cochineal bug, a type of beetle. Ultramarine blue of the best purity and quality is obtained from the semi-precious lapis lazuli stone, and bladder green formerly was obtained from the bladder of certain animals.

Currently there are a number of chemical tints and colors, and in comparison to natural pigments, they offer a great difference in subtlety and balance.

Nature is undoubtedly a great source of inspiration, as shown in this photo showing the integration of several elements in their natural environment.

A wall aged with water glazes to create an effect of worn antique fresco.

Color in history

Color has also been used as a sign of social position, since pigments are priced according to their color; price is determined by purity and by the difficulty of obtaining certain colors.

A deep green may be eight times more costly than a beige. Blue, royal yellow, and some reds and oranges are colors whose pure pigments can be very costly.

In many cultures, colors have even come to represent life and death, and they have characterized different styles throughout history, such as neoclassicism's Adam's blue. Oxblood red was widely used in decorating in the eighteenth century. Red has always been a color associated with luxury and richness, and it has produced great impact in combination with other colors.

People are still investigating the role of color in history to find its origins; there is a wealth of information on this topic in books from the seventeenth to the nineteenth centuries.

A palette of colors

In painting, the magnificent combination of colors formed by the rainbow by means of the breakdown of white light can be reduced to three basic colors: yellow, magenta, and blue. Different mixtures of these three basic or primary colors can yield any color. Sometimes it's adequate to mix just two of them.

The colors produced in that way are termed secondary colors. Tertiary colors produced by further mixing constitute a broad palette of mixtures and color in an endless number of hues and values that make up the chromatic circle.

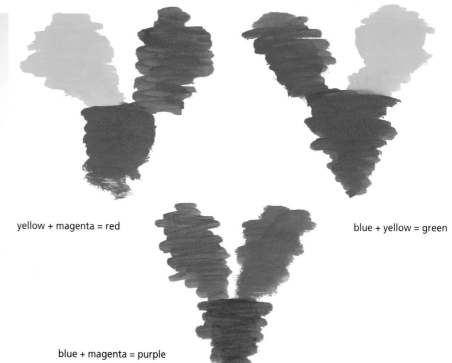

yellow + magenta = red

blue + yellow = green

blue + magenta = purple

Cold and warm colors

If we divide up the chromatic circle, we get a group of colors and hues that are known as cold colors; basically, these are the most subdued colors. The different hues of blues, grays, and soft purples convey a smooth, relaxing visual effect.

Warm colors are the brighter ones, cheerful and impressive, yet at the same time cozy. These are the spectrum of yellows, reds, and oranges. There are also variations according to the proportions of color that are mixed together. If you add a greater amount of purple to a red, it is transformed into a cold color; if you add some red to a blue, it changes into a warm hue.

Cold colors.

Aged colors

Many finishes in decorative painting involve using bright and luminous colors, and then giving them an appearance of age to suggest the passage of time; these colors are often used to create that impression. All the earthy colors, purples, browns, grays, and blacks, help create the aged appearance that many objects have.

Warm colors.

Blacks

Black goes well with colors such as gold, silver, and white, which set off its chromatic value. It is always a difficult color to apply on large surfaces, since it absorbs light and inspires sadness. That's why it's best to use it sparingly, for details, or in other very subtle applications. It's not a good idea to use it to darken other colors, since it only dirties them. In the chromatic scale, black represents the absence of light and color.

Blacks in the artist's palette have different properties that are obtainable through different mixtures; for example, a smoky black is a cold color, but an ivory black is a warmer color. Different mixtures using ultramarine blue and carmine lacquer can produce some interesting hues.

An assortment of blacks.

Grays

Pearl gray, smoke gray, and silver are ambiguous and mysterious. There are also some warm grays based on mixtures of pinks and greens, and cold grays obtained by mixing blues and umbers.

The easiest way to get a gray is to mix white and black, but the result is very simple and without character. It's better to create more appealing hues of gray through different mixtures of colors and adding white to them.

Grays can appear cold, but depending on how they're mixed, they can create a warm effect that's neutral at the same time. Using pinks, beiges, and whites, you can come up with various tints of gray and some very artistic decorative effects. Also, since it's a neutral color, it can be combined with practically all other colors.

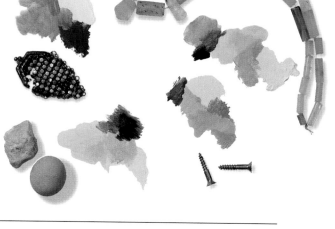

An assortment of grays.

Whites

White is associated with light and purity; it always plays an important role in decoration. It mixes with all colors to intensify or to subdue their impact. White is a shade, and in reality it's erroneous to call it a color, since it's a combination of all the colors. Sometimes painters mix in small amounts of sienna to create very subtle hues; this breaks up the white and creates shades like ivory or a white with a touch of pink. Mixing natural umber with white produces an off-white. Pure whites include titanium white, which is opaque and covers well; very transparent zinc white; and lead white, which is more durable and much faster drying than the others.

When mixed with a small amount of color, the off-whites produce an infinity of hues and tones.

An assortment of whites.

Reds

The broad range of earthy reds, from dark terra-cottas to pink and bright oranges, is obtained from iron oxides. These colors have been around since prehistoric times, when they were used to reproduce hunting scenes and rituals on cave walls. In some cultures, such as in China, the color red represents happiness and good luck; it also stands for passion and anger, and is symbolic of danger and fire. No color is more distinctive than red.

In decorating, red has been used to suggest richness and abundance. The pure, bright red pigments in red paints were very costly. Red should be used in moderation, since it can come across as aggressive; but in combination with other colors or hues, it's warm and full of life, though no less striking. Reds in more subdued shades such as earthy reds, ochres, and burnt siennas are excellent colors for use in decorating. Additionally, they combine very well with grays, blues, and greens.

When reds are mixed carefully with natural sienna, burnt sienna, and yellow ochre, their bright color is softened, producing shades that are ideal for decorating everything from objects to walls.

Their best effect when used straight is in combination with the color gold.

An assortment of reds.

Yellows

The spectrum of yellows is very broad, ranging from ochres to brilliant China yellow. It's a torrid and rich color that evokes warmth and the sun's rays; yellow reflects light and makes spaces seem larger. It can give rise to endless shades: corn, brass, topaz, and earthy golden yellows. All shades of ochres are used in abundance for decorating.

Many shades of yellow can be made by mixing it with white, burnt umber, or burnt sienna; reds produce orange shades. Yellow intensifies or nearly disappears as a function of natural or artificial light. It's a good idea to try out mixtures of shades before making a final choice.

An assortment of yellows.

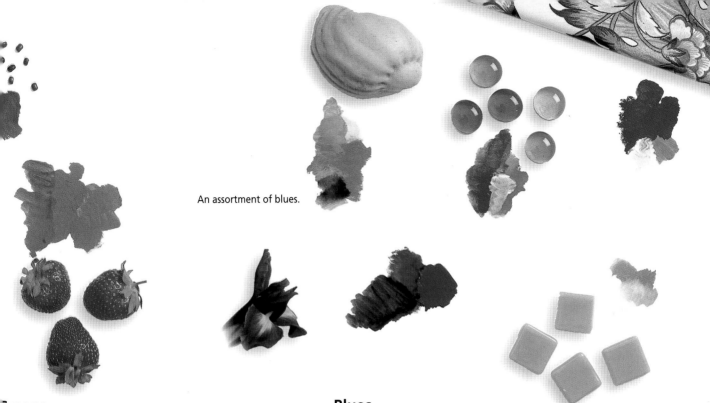

An assortment of blues.

Greens

The color green represents harmony; it's the result of combining yellow and blue, and it inevitably suggests nature's landscape colors such as olive green, mint, and apple. Mineral greens include emerald, malachite, and jade.

Green is the national color of England. Various shades of green have always been used in decorating; they communicate peace and tranquillity, and some tones are very elegant, suggesting refinement and simplicity as they echo the shades of the natural world. Greens have frequently been used on furniture and accessories, but also on walls and in fabrics. Green is very versatile in soft shades; but bright, intense greens also defined a style of decorating salons in the Napoleonic empire.

When the gray Scandinavian greens and the traditional bottle greens of Holland are applied to exteriors, they demonstrate the great variety of shades this color can take.

The warmest shades are made by adding a greater quantity of yellow; when greens are mixed with more blue, they appear colder. The complementary color is red; different mixes combine with an infinity of colors—whites, pinks, grays, for example—to produce very attractive effects.

Blues

Blue really gives an impression of broad expanses such as space, the sky, and the sea. It's a very common color in nature; it's peaceful and refreshing. It's a restful color that is often used in bedrooms; it's also used in bathrooms, since it suggests an aquatic environment. It's not always a cold color, since its many shades range from a broad spectrum of violet to pale blue, underwater blue, indigo, and Prussian blue. In times past, blue was obtained from indigo, a plant or organic dye. Ground lapis lazuli, a precious mineral, yielded an intense but very expensive blue.

Blue harmonizes well with any number of colors in all their shades, especially with the ranges of yellows and ochres, as well as with whites.

Blues made on the basis of ultramarine blue create a warmer impression, since they have a bit of red in them. Mixtures using white and Prussian blue or cobalt yield colder shades. Azure blue in combination with white and ultramarine reproduces the intensity of the sky.

An assortment of greens.

Application

The choice of color and effect for decorating a room or space is a consideration that needs to be thought through carefully in light of some basic requirements. In addition to the dimensions and the shape of the space to be decorated, it's crucial to consider the type of illumination, whether natural or artificial, since that has a bearing on the final results. You should also consider if the room will be used more in the day than the night, and for what purpose—whether it's a bedroom, a dining room, or a study. All these details will help ensure that the color choice and the effect created are the ones desired.

Horizontal or vertical stripes accentuate the visual impression of height or width. Used in the right ways, they enlarge or reduce spaces. On wainscoting such as in the photo, the bright colors can liven up dark and unattractive walkways.

The use of bold and intense colors can sometimes be the key to creating pleasing effects. The blue vaults and walls of the archeological museum of Pamplona, Spain, are proof of how important color can be in creating impressions.

Proportion

The dimensions of the space to be decorated determine the type of effect that can be created and the colors that can be used. A wall is like a blank canvas that can be handled in different ways, and the effects created on it will determine the overall visual experience. The proportions of a room can be altered visually to create particular effects; stripes and friezes are horizontal divisions that highlight effects or defects. In extremely high spaces, horizontal stripes give the impression that the walls aren't so tall. If ceilings in an area that's too high are painted in a dark color, the space seems more cozy.

Sometimes in areas that are too low, painting vertical or horizontal stripes creates an impression of greater or lesser height. It's truly amazing how a space can be modified according to the color or the effect used in decorating it.

Light

It's really important to take into account the lighting of a space; this is subject to some established rules. Small rooms, specially if they are dark, should be decorated with light and luminous colors to create an impression of spaciousness and keep them from being stifling; but this is not always the case, since decorating such spaces with bright colors and accepting their limitations can create a brilliance that compensates for the lack of space. The dimensions of a room can be altered visually by applying the right color. Warm oranges, yellow, and red are hues that create a cozy and intimate space; used boldly, they seem to advance, and they reduce the size of a room. On the other hand, cold colors seem to recede, and they give an impression of spaciousness. If there's not much natural light, strong colors intensify and increase its effect and richness.

Spaces that have lots of light are ideal for light colors that accentuate the spacious atmosphere. Neutral colors and different pastel shades can lend vitality to such spaces.

Lighting is very important in giving a room atmosphere, and different effects to color. Similarly, the right application of natural or artificial light can intensify or soften color. In this room, artificial light creates a cozy and intimate atmosphere and reinforces the earthy red color of the walls.

Texture

The texture of the surfaces should also be considered; smooth, matte, and porous surfaces absorb light and appear lighter in color; glossy or bright surfaces reflect light, creating an impression of heightened colors.

Some painting techniques can also be used to mask imperfections in the surface, and if the right technique is used, a surface that's in poor condition can be transformed and take on a stylish appearance. On the other hand, other techniques require smooth or well finished surfaces to achieve good results with the intended effect. Many finishes can be applied in the same way on walls and objects: moldings and architectural details can be decorated using techniques that transform them completely through color and texture. If texture is added to new, smooth surfaces, the final finish can be enriched, thereby giving added value to the treated surface.

A false molding and a stenciled frieze in the Victorian style are textured effects created on a surface using oil techniques. The combination of ochres, yellows, and terra-cottas produces a classic and cozy finish.

chapter

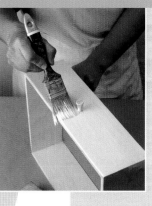

Basic preparations used in decorative painting

Decorative painting is a great resource in the world of decorating, and sometimes lots of practice is needed to master the various techniques involved. To begin with, it's essential to be familiar with the mixes and the little secrets of each technique. It's also necessary to be able to distinguish among the different types of products, both traditional and modern, that are available in today's marketplace. We'll now examine in detail how to prepare the various compositions and, in each case, how to use them simply and practically. We'll also stress how to prepare each of the surfaces to be decorated. This chapter is of great importance in acquiring the knowledge necessary to enter the world of decorative painting, where there are no limits if you use your creativity and imagination.

Surface preparation

There is a great variety of materials that are used in decorative painting techniques. Their preparation, purity, priming, and the application of an adequate base coat are factors necessary to achieving success with any technique. You have to consider the condition of the surface; a new one will be treated differently than an older one, or one that has been treated previously.

Walls

Walls can be the most challenging surfaces to work with because of their size. There are several things to consider that affect how walls are treated.

Before starting to decorate walls, you have to be sure that there is no dampness present; otherwise all your work will be ruined. Once any damage has been repaired, you can continue with surface preparation (see chart on page 33).

Fillers

Stores offer a wide variety of ready-to-use fillers. All-purpose fillers are used on many types of surfaces, but there are also different compounds designed specifically for concrete, wood, metal, plastic, ceramic, and so forth. They are applied in very thin layers, allowing adequate drying time between successive layers, since some kinds of filler, especially the traditional plasters, may otherwise crack. Currently there are also plasters available that contain an acrylic that makes them more durable, elastic, and flexible.

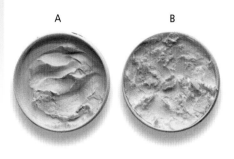

A   B

Ready-to-use commercial filler (A). Synthetic auto-body filler (B).

1- Use a scraper to remove traces of old paint when repairing chipped walls.

2- Cover cracks in walls with plaster. After the plaster has dried, smooth the surface by sanding.

3- Before starting work, remove dust from walls to improve adhesion of the base coat.

WALL PREPARATION

WALLS	CLEANING	PREPARATION	PRIMING	BASE PAINT
Plastered, unpainted, old or new	Remove dust from surface with brush or broom.	Fill small cracks with all-purpose filler. Fill large holes with plaster. Sand lightly once dry.	**Old plaster:** All-purpose oleosynthetic sealer; let dry 24 hours. **New plaster:** Be sure it's dry. All-purpose oleosynthetic sealer; let dry 24 hours.	**Finish:** Two coats of flat acrylic paint applied with brush or roller. **With water-based paints:** Two coats of satin-finish acrylic paint applied with brush or roller. **With oil paints:** Two coats of alkyd satin-finish paint.
Painted, new or old	Dust surface. Wash with warm water and detergent and let dry. Sand or scrape lightly to remove traces of old paint.	Fill small cracks and dents with all-purpose filler. Use plaster to fill large holes. Once dry, sand lightly.	**New:** Acrylic primer-sealer. **Old:** All-purpose oleosynthetic primer-sealer.	See Plaster Walls.
Papered, new or old	**New:** Clean with damp rag to remove dirt and dust. **Old:** Thoroughly soak paper with hot water applied with brush. When it starts to come loose, remove all paper with a scraper used crosswise.	**New:** Plaster small dents over paper. **Old:** Sand lightly; apply all-purpose filler to cracks, and plaster to large holes.	**New:** Apply all-purpose primer-sealer over paper in good condition. **Old:** Apply oleo-synthetic primer-sealer.	See Plaster Walls.

Base coat

There are various types of paints that are used to prepare and cover substrates. Acrylic paints, which are porous, are used particularly for substrates such as walls; they are moderately durable. They come in flat, satin, and gloss finishes. Satin-finish paints are best as a base for creating special effects with water-based paints. These finishes must be protected with varnish. Acrylic paints are the most durable; once dry they are water resistant and can be used with aging finishes, or as smooth finish coats. They also are available in flat, satin, and glossy finishes. Acrylic artists' paints, which are used to paint details or pictures by hand, are higher quality. Enamels are very durable paints similar to lacquers. You can buy water-based enamels that dilute and clean up with water, but whose characteristics are nearly identical to the very hard and durable finishes of oil-based enamels. Turpentine is used to clean up and dilute oil-based enamels.

Vinyl paint (A). Water-based enamel (B). Acrylic paint (C). Oil-based enamel (D).

Other surfaces

No matter what type of surface you intend to decorate, whether old or new, you have to clean it carefully of all dust, left-over wax, and old paint. Any left-over dirt or grease will interfere with proper adhesion of the primer and paint you use in decorating.

Primer-sealers

There are many products available for sealing surfaces, such as sizing, gum lacquer, and even more economical, PVA and latex.

The industry has conducted ongoing research, and it's come up with specific products suited to every kind of job. Oleosynthetic primers are very durable; they are used on almost every type of surface. They clean up and dilute with turpentine. Acrylic primers are lighter, but they're also more durable; they're very easy to use since they are diluted with water. With a very few exceptions, the newest generation of sealers are all-purpose, and they adhere to difficult and nonporous surfaces such as steel and ceramic. They are diluted with turpentine, and are very durable.

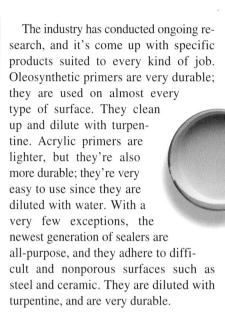

C

B

A

All-purpose oleosynthetic primer (A).
Acrylic primer (B).
All-purpose primer (C).

Plastic

Wash the surface with hot water and soap and let dry well. With medium-grit sandpaper, sand lightly to roughen the surface a little. This helps the primer adhere better. There are primers specially made for nonporous materials like plastic, and they adhere very strongly.

1- Sand the surface of the plastic to improve adhesion of the primer.

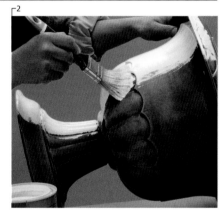

2- Apply special primer-sealer for plastic.

Wood

For good results it's essential to clean and prepare the wood properly. A durable finish always depends on adequate preparation. New wood presents no particular problem. If you have to decorate wood that's in bad condition or that has old paint on it, consult the chart on page 35.

1- Sand the surface carefully and remove all traces of dust.

2- Apply primer-sealer to the wood, brushing it on evenly with the grain.

Metals

New metals free of rust and in good condition can be cleaned with alcohol to remove any traces of dirt, dust, grease, and so forth.

There are many types of primer for metals; some of them also prevent rust.

1- Clean with alcohol to eliminate all dirt. Let dry.

2- Apply a thin coat of metal primer.

CLEANING AND PREPARATION OF OTHER SURFACES

MATERIAL	CLEANING	PREPARATION	PRIMER TYPE	BASE COAT TYPE
New wood	Sand lightly with the grain using medium-grit sandpaper. Remove all dust.	Use plastic wood to fill holes and cracks; let dry. Sand lightly with medium-grit sandpaper and remove sanding dust.	**New or old:** Apply all-purpose acrylic primer; let dry and sand lightly.	**For smooth finishes:** Two coats of flat or satin-finish acrylic paint applied with brush or roller. **For effects with water-based paint:** Two coats of acrylic satin-finish paint applied with brush or roller. **For effects with oil-based paint:** Two coats of synthetic satin-finish paint applied with roller.
Painted or old wood	Wash surface with warm water, soap, and a few drops of ammonia. Let dry and sand lightly with fine sandpaper.		**Painted:** Apply all-purpose alkyd primer; let dry and sand lightly.	
Plastic, PVC, fiberglass, and similar materials	Wash well with hot water and soap. Let dry and sand with medium-grit sandpaper. Remove dust.	Fill holes and cracks with special auto-body filler. Let dry and sand lightly with medium-grit sandpaper.	Apply all-purpose primer-sealer or special primer for plastics and nonporous surfaces. Let dry 24 hours and sand lightly.	Depending on the desired effect, apply base coat as directed in box that specifies type of base coat.
Steel and other metals	**Old:** Remove all rust with a wire brush or scouring pad and sand lightly. **New:** Clean with alcohol, let dry and sand lightly.	Fill holes and cracks with auto-body filler. Let dry and sand.	Apply a coat of rust-proofing and let dry two hours. Then apply a coat of universal sealer or sealer for metals. Sand lightly.	Depending on the desired effect, apply base paint as directed in box that indicates type of base coat.
Terra-cotta and plaster: large and small objects	Sand lightly with fine sandpaper and remove dust with a dry brush or a rag.	Fill holes and cracks with all-purpose filler. Let dry and remove dust.	Apply a coat of acrylic primer-sealer. Let dry four hours and sand lightly.	Depending on the desired effect, apply base paint as directed in the box that indicates type of base coat.
Styrofoam	Sand lightly with fine-grit sandpaper and remove dust.	Fill holes and dents with diluted latex filler; apply with artist's brush; let dry and sand.	Apply coat of acrylic primer-sealer; let dry two hours. Apply a second coat; let dry and sand.	Depending on the desired effect, apply base coat as directed in box that indicates type of base coat.
Ceramics	Wash surface thoroughly with hot water and soap and let dry.	Fill cracks and holes with all-purpose filler.	Apply a coat of all-purpose primer-sealer or special primer-sealer for non-porous surfaces. Let dry 24 hours. Apply a second coat if necessary.	Depending on the desired effect, apply base coat as directed in box that indicates type of base coat.

Types and preparation of paints

There are essentially two large families in which paints are classified: water paints, whose pigments and binders are soluble in water; and oil paints, whose pigments and binders are dissolved with turpentine.

It's presumed that readers are already familiar with the basic characteristics of each of these. We can thus recognize that the choice of paint will probably be dictated by the type of binder, which is what holds the paint together.

Pigments

Pigments are materials in powdered form that have the ability to impart color when mixed with more or less fluid substances. Mixed with binder and diluted with substances that render them liquid, they form paints. One type is organic pigments derived from plants, animals, some calcinations of various materials, or the boiling of certain seeds. Inorganic pigments are mineral ones; the most ancient and natural ones are types of earth, ochres, siennas, umbers, and others. There are others that are designated as artificial, since they are produced by chemical reactions on metals, such as red oxide, yellow iron oxide, and others.

Vegetable pigments come from some plants or the resins derived from them; examples include indigo blue, which is obtained from the indigo plant, and crimson, which comes from madder root.

Pigments of primary colors.

Paints

The great variety of paints and the different types that are available in the marketplace may sometimes be confusing. The best idea is to ask the advice of the professionals in a specialty shop, explaining the type of results you hope to obtain.

Vinyl paints

There's a broad spectrum of shades and colors of vinyl paints available on the market; most are used for walls and large surfaces, so they are quite reasonably priced. They are composed mainly of the color provided by the pigment dissolved in water and the binder, which in this case is polyvinyl acetate, commonly known as acrylic latex. Water is used to dilute this white, milky emulsion.

Real latex is the milky juice that flows from cuts on the trunks of certain plants, but nowadays latex is produced artificially by chemical processes.

The main characteristics of this paint are elasticity and consistency. It can be bought in matte and satin finishes.

Preparing vinyl paint

Dissolve one part pigment in three parts water until the coloring is entirely dissolved. Add one part latex and stir until it's well mixed in with the coloring. To begin mixing, add teaspoons of Spanish white; this will turn the liquid into a fairly thick emulsion without altering its color.

This is the way you would make vinyl paint at home.

In large paint factories, these mixtures are made by machines so that large quantities of paint are more homogenous.

Latex, pigment, and Spanish white mixed with water.

Acrylic paints

Acrylic is another binder (also known as copolymer acrylic); it's a milky white, and it is more durable and long-lasting than vinyls. Acrylic paint is available from manufacturers in a great variety of colors. It is used for painting surfaces that have to withstand severe abrasion, such as children's furniture and kitchen furniture. It's too expensive for large surfaces, and it's not well suited to custom finishes with glazes, since its chief characteristic is repelling anything that's put over it. In small quantities it's fine for freehand finishes and as a base for aging patinas. Acrylic paints are available in industrial sizes and in containers for artists. They dry fast, are durable and flexible, and are impervious to water once dry. They come in flat and satin finishes.

• Preparing acrylic paint
Add the pigment to the acrylic emulsion until it becomes fairly thick.

A mixture of pigment and acrylic binder.

Oil paints

These are greasy paints whose binder is a vegetable oil that's capable of drying. Olive oil, for example, won't work, since it doesn't dry. The oil most commonly used is linseed; this may be boiled to speed up drying time, or raw, which dries more slowly. This oil is derived from the seeds of the flax plant.

• Preparing oil paint
You can make a simple type of oil paint at home using only linseed oil, essence of turpentine, and pigment.

In a glass or porcelain container, mix the linseed oil and pigment, then stir to the consistency of raw dough. Keep stirring and add more raw linseed oil to thin.

Add essence of turpentine until the paint becomes viscous and fluid. If there are any lumps, you can remove them with a strainer.

Currently there are different types of oil paints available in the marketplace. Normally we find them labeled as alkyd or enamel paints; they are manufactured using a very sophisticated process, and they are very durable once dry.

A mixture of boiled linseed oil, pigment, and turpentine.

Samples of vinyl paint.

Samples of alkyd paint.

Samples of acrylic paint.

Glazes

Glazes are transparent paints that are used to create different effects in decorative painting. They can be oil- or water-based.

Mix half the water with the pigment to make a uniform solution. The amount of pigment will depend in part on the type and color. You can use less with dark colors and more with light ones.

Use the rest of the water to dissolve the quantity of latex so that there are no lumps. Once the two mixtures are thoroughly dissolved, mix them together and stir well so that the pigment and the latex are perfectly integrated.

Pigments have a tendency to settle to the bottom, and it's a good idea to keep a brush on hand to stir the mixture and preserve the same color intensity.

Water-based glazes

These produce a very attractive finish and can be used for a wide variety of decorative effects. Their only disadvantage is their very short drying time, which requires you to work quickly.

• **Preparation**
Materials and amounts:
1 part pigment
1 part latex
4 parts water

Preparing a water glaze.

Oil-based glazes

These are the best paints for imitating marble and wood grain. The resulting finish can be either glossy or satin.

• **Preparation**
Materials and amounts:
1 part raw linseed oil
2 parts turpentine
$\frac{1}{2}$ part oil color or pigment
5% drier

Dissolve the quantity of tube coloring or pigment in turpentine. Add the quantity of linseed oil to the mixture, followed by the drier.

Oil paints have a very long drying time; adding drier to the mixture shortens it. The maximum amount of drier should be about 5% of the total mixture; if you add too much, the results might change and the mixture might not dry at all.

You can check the color when the mixture is ready; if it's too transparent and lacking in color, you can add more until you get the color you want without sacrificing transparency.

Preparing oil glaze.

Oil-based glazes with varnish

These are basically colored varnish, but to lengthen the drying time, we add a little linseed oil. These dry more quickly than oil glazes, and they're used for countless attractive finishes. They are applied to large and small surfaces, and they're used for finishing furniture. They are used on surfaces over a base coat of satin-finish oil-based paint.

• **Preparation**
Materials and amounts:
1 part flat oil-based varnish
$\frac{1}{2}$ part raw linseed oil
$\frac{1}{2}$ part turpentine
oil coloring or pigment

Dissolve the oil color or the pigment in the turpentine and add the linseed oil and the varnish; stir the whole mixture well to create a homogeneous solution.

Preparing oil glaze with varnish.

Others

The following explanations focus on creating different decorative effects. As long as you mix the right formula for the different materials, the effects of oxidation and aging are fairly easy to create on the surfaces of objects and walls. The results can be striking.

Preparing iron sulfate

Iron sulfate is a product that can easily be obtained in drugstores; it's often used as a fertilizer for plants that have an iron deficiency. It has a very high oxidizing capability and produces very decorative finishes on objects. It comes as a fine

sand or in larger lumps. Dissolve one part iron sulfate in one part water. It doesn't dissolve entirely, and it can also be used as a fine sand in noncrystalline form to lend a little texture.

Preparing iron sulfate.

Sample piece treated with iron sulfate.

Preparing an asphaltum and wax patina

Bitumen of Judea, or asphaltum, is the classic glaze for aging. It's a fossil resin, and its name comes from ancient deposits in the Jordan Valley.

It's a brilliant black, and it dries fairly quickly. That's why we mix it with wax so it can be worked longer and in different shades.

Preparing a patina of asphaltum and wax.

Sample piece treated with asphaltum and wax patina.

Gum lacquer stain

Gum lacquer is a resin made by an insect, the lacquer cochineal; it's gathered from the branches where the creature lives. It comes in the form of flakes, and it's quite clear once the color is removed; its original color is a reddish orange. It's dissolved in alcohol to make a liquid, and it's available in prepared form in specialty shops. It is used to waterproof and protect gilding.

It can be bought with added coloring for use in creating decorative effects.

The amount of pigment may vary according to the brightness desired. Add ½ tablespoon of coffee to 300 ml of liquid

Gum lacquer stain.

gum lacquer; more can be added to brighten the color. The mixture must remain very liquid.

Use alcohol to wash brushes and other tools used in applying gum lacquer.

Sample piece stained with gum lacquer.

Traditional techniques

Throughout the ages people have experimented with different materials, such as binders, to make paint; many of the formulas used ingredients that were easily obtainable locally. Some of the results are still useful, since the passage of time has demonstrated their durability and continued good condition. In the following passages we set forth a few very old formulas that are widely used today by artisans and restorers to make various types of paint.

Egg tempera

The origins of this technique are very old, but research indicates that it has been used since the tenth century. In the Middle Ages it was used for painting on wood. There are some impressive Gothic altar pieces on gilded backgrounds where this technique was used. A long list of artists, including Fra Angelico, Piero de la Francesca, and Botticelli, used this procedure for their works painted on wood. It was revived in the nineteenth century at the hand of such painters as the Frenchman Gustave Moreau.

Egg tempera consists primarily of an emulsion of egg yolk diluted with water to the right consistency, to which a small amount of resin or linseed oil is added. The albumin contained in the yolk makes the paint insoluble in water once it's dry. It's essential to follow the indicated order for mixing the various ingredients; otherwise the paint won't come out right.

1- Given the antiquity of egg tempera, there are various formulas for preparing it, but a good mixture would be as follows: the yolk of one egg, boiled or distilled water, and mastic varnish or damar.

2- Separate the yolk entirely from the white; pop the egg yolk with your index finger and thumb and remove the entire membrane that surrounds the yolk, leaving behind only the liquid.

3- Next, use the shell of the egg for measuring, and add one-half part of mastic varnish to one part of egg yolk, stirring gently.
This is a technique half-way between oils and water-based paints; you can also use linseed oil instead of varnish.

4- Then, while continuing to stir, add two parts distilled water to the mixture. Keep stirring until the mixture is totally homogeneous; finally, add the desired pigment to give it color.
The best surface for use with this formula is wood previously prepared with a primer coat of rabbit-skin glue and Spanish white.

Casein tempera

's difficult to pinpoint when any type f material was first used to produce different kinds of paint. In all ages, people ave experimented with different liqd or sticky substances to bind their aints, including various plant resins, ums, milk, egg, and animal fats. Sev-al studies indicate that some of the aintings in Pompeii were done with ca-ein. In the fifteenth century, there was ention of a glue made from cheese and me, which was probably a medieval quivalent of modern calcic casein glue. merican colonists painted their furni-re and walls with lime casein, since the ngredients were easy to obtain. Nowa-ays casein paint can be bought in spe-ialty shops; it must be kept in a cool lace or refrigerated. It's a durable, flat aint.

1- Water, powdered casein, and ammonia. Casein is a protein obtained from curdled milk. The curd is separated from the whey and left to dry; once dry, it's ground. Since it's insoluble in water, it's very resistant to atmospheric changes. To dissolve it you have to add some lime, carbonate of ammonia, or ammonia. Nowadays casein powder is manufactured commercially.

3- Then add ½ ounce (15 g) of carbonate of ammonia or a few drops of ammonia, stirring vigorously until the mixture thickens to the consistency of honey and is free of lumps. This produces a strong glue; thinned in proportions of one part glue to three parts water, it's a tempera well suited to mixing with pigment to produce a colored paint.

2- Soak about 2 ounces (50 g) of casein for two to three hours in a cup (¼ L) of water. Stir occasionally.

Gesso

esso was used by the ancient Egyp-ans. It has been used as a base for gold eaf, and it has a long history in priming nd preparing furniture for decoration. his primer produces a smooth and po-ous surface when applied in layers and anded between coats. It's quite easy to repare, but nowadays you can buy an quivalent product in specialty shops.

1- Soak about 5 ounces (150 g) of powdered rabbit-skin glue in 1 quart (1L) of boiled or distilled water for 24 hours. Sizing is available in powdered or sheet form; if you have sheet sizing, use three sheets per quart/liter of water. When the granules swell up, but before they disintegrate, heat them in a double boiler, stirring with a wooden spoon, until they are completely dissolved. It's important to keep the glue from boiling; otherwise, it will lose its strength.

2- When the granules are entirely gone, strain or filter the glue through a sieve or nylon mesh to remove impurities and lumps.

3- Next, add some Spanish white or chalk to the glue as a whitener. Keep stirring the mixture over the double boiler until you get an emulsion that looks like paint. This preparation, like all others made with organic glues, deteriorates after a few days, especially in warm places. It must be kept in a cool spot or in the refrigerator, and replaced when it starts to deteriorate. While the mixture is still hot, filter it again to remove lumps. Keep in mind that if the glue is of good quality, it will harden when it cools. To use it, you have to return it to a liquid state by heating it in a double boiler.

Finishes

Finishes that use varnishes and waxes are indispensable in making sure that a job that's taken a lot of time and effort lasts as long as possible and stands up to scratches, dust, and hard knocks. This step should be part of every project; it will keep lots of extensive and excellent work from being ruined because of a careless finish. There are also various materials that can be used to create special effects and finish off a job nicely.

Waxes

Wax finishes impart to a treated surface a very pleasant smoothness to the touch and a gentle sheen. They can be applied for protection directly over enamel, paint, or lacquer, but they will provide better durability and protection for the surface when applied on top of several coats of varnish. There are several types of wax: virgin beeswax, synthetic silicone wax, and others. They can be dyed with powdered pigments, asphaltum, and oils. For such mixtures, it's preferable to use uncolored wax with no additional oils, since they would change the drying properties. Wax is applied to brighten and protect surfaces; once dry, it is buffed with soft cloths or with fine steel wool. It can be removed with turpentine. When mixed with asphaltum, it's very useful in creating aged finishes; in combination with white pigment or calcic wax, it's used for decorative effects.

Metallic waxes

Metallic waxes are available on the market in a broad spectrum of colors from different shades of gold to silver and pewter. Because they cover well, they are very useful for touching up gilded pieces. They also create metallic effects when used as patinas. They are applied in small amounts so that the effects don't look too artificial, and on top of varnish, they can be buffed once dry to make them shine.

Sample metallic waxes. Pewter (A), old gold (B), yellow gold (C), silver (D) copper (E).

Sample waxes. Uncolored wax (A), wax with asphaltum (B), liquid wax (C), calcic wax (D), powdered wax (E), colored wax (F), beeswax (G).

Varnishes

Varnish is without doubt the best product for protecting treated surfaces; it creates a moisture barrier and adds quality and depth to the special effects of the finish. There are so many varieties of varnishes available that you have to know how to choose the best one for each type of job. Essentially they are divided into three groups: oil-based varnishes, water-based or acrylic varnishes, and alcohol-based varnishes.

Types of varnishes

• Oil-based varnish
Synthetic varnish, which is an oil-based varnish composed of synthetic resins and oils, is thicker in consistency than acrylic varnish. Although it's the most transparent of the industrial varnishes, over time and on white surfaces, it tends to yellow.

Varnish should be used diluted for the first coats; this protects the surface more effectively and keeps it from looking as if it were coated in plastic. A surface is best protected with three light coats of varnish followed by a single thicker coat.

The first coat is a solution of 70% varnish and 30% oil of turpentine or turpentine. For the second coat, a solution of 80% varnish and 20% oil of turpentine is used; if three or more coats are called for, 90% varnish and 10% oil of turpentine is used.

This type of varnish is also tinted with oils and pigments to prepare glazes. It's available in flat, satin, and glossy finishes, and is soluble in oil of turpentine.

Transparent oil-based varnish (A). Transparent polyurethane varnish (B). Transparent acrylic varnish (C). Mahogany-colored polyurethane varnish (D).

• Polyurethane varnish
This is a very durable and long-lasting varnish. It's used to protect surfaces that are subjected to hard wear. It tends to yellow more than oil-based varnish, but it's much more resistant to wear. It's also used diluted with oil of turpentine; several coats are applied with adequate drying time between coats. It has a dark caramel color, but it's almost transparent once dry; it comes in flat, satin, and glossy finishes. It's applied with a soft brush, or with a soft roller on large surfaces.

• Acrylic varnish
Acrylic varnishes are composed of acrylic or vinyl resins in a water solution. They dry quickly and are quite transparent. They are not quite as durable as oil varnishes. They are applied to both large and small areas. Latex or PVA diluted with water, like water-based varnish, also serves a protective function on surfaces that don't require much protection. It's dissolved in water and can be either satin or glossy, depending on the amount of acrylic resin it contains. Although opaque when applied, it becomes clear when it dries.

• Alcohol varnish
Gum lacquer is considered an alcohol varnish. It is used in some painting techniques, especially in restoring furniture, and as a protective varnish for gilding. It's diluted with alcohol and is available in different shades; it can also be dyed with pigments. Gum lacquer is applied with an applicator or a soft brush.

Aerosol varnish

• Aerosol varnish
Some companies offer varnish in aerosol containers. It's a good choice in cases where applying varnish with a brush could drag or spoil a special effect. You have to follow carefully the manufacturer's directions for use, and you must work in a well-ventilated area.

Whatever the type of varnish selected, you must remember to work in a clean area, since varnish is very susceptible to all kinds of lint, and especially to dust, which will stick to the surface while the varnish is still wet. The brushes you use must also be clean.

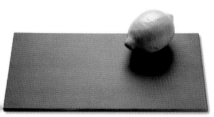

Sample of a flat varnish.

Sample of a satin varnish.

Sample of a glossy varnish.

Water techniques

There are many techniques in decorative painting, but they can be divided into two basic categories: water and oil. Water techniques include all those where the pigments and binders used are water-soluble. They are easy to apply either as a base coat or a glaze to produce various special effects. They dry quickly, and all the materials and brushes used in applying them are cleaned up with water and soap.

On the other hand, disadvantages include the difficulty of creating certain effects due to the quick drying and the brief time available for working with them. Also, the finishes have to be protected with varnish to make them more durable.

Decorating with water techniques

Techniques using water are considered to be the oldest, since this medium is very basic, easy to work with, and economical; also, in combination with different binders, it's possible to make very long-lasting paints, which may remain in good condition over time. The techniques described in this book, some of which are very basic, are the starting point of all finishes used in decorative painting. Every example, whether used alone or in conjunction with others, makes it possible to achieve a special decorative finish that lends a personal touch and reflects an individual style.

Applications

Applications are very diverse, and can be used for decorating large areas such as interior and exterior walls, for decorating furniture, and on large and small objects.

Acrylics are used in flat colors for base coats; you can find these ready-made in a broad spectrum of colors in specialty shops, or you can prepare them yourself using pigments, and adjust the shades with all-purpose colorings. Different finishes—flat, satin, and glossy— are available, but the glossy finishes are not suited to use as a base coat for creating special effects.

This decoration, done with water glazes, makes for a pleasant combination of red ochres, bluish grays, and mustard colors.

Decorative effects

lso referred to as decorative and faux nishes, these are used to create more aborate and sophisticated effects than a ain, smooth finish. Many of these decrative effects are produced with glazes, irly transparent paints diluted with wa-r in various proportions.

Water techniques reduce to a mini-um the offensive fumes that other aints give off, but the possible decora-ve effects are more limited, and they ave to be produced more quickly be-ause they dry quite fast. You can buy roducts designed to slow down drying me and make it easier to work with ese techniques. You can do many things with these techniques, but for centuries their secrets were known only to professionals and artisans. Since this type of painting has become fashionable once again, some of the techniques have been revived.

The many effects that can be created by applying glazes with different uten-sils—brushes, pieces of plastic, rags, sponges, combs, and so forth—produce very different and special looks and tex-tures that lend an individual character and personality to the environment, walls, and furniture.

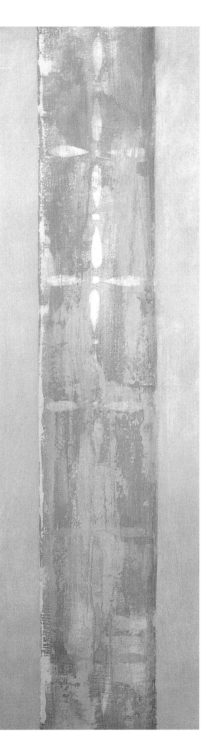

Frieze created with water technique. Superimposed water glazes of different colors and an appearance of deterioration combine to form a decoration in medieval style.

Where to apply

inishes and effects with water tech-iques are applied onto practically all irfaces, as long as they are prepared roperly. Effects are created with light bats of satin-finish acrylic paint; this chnique is best suited for special ef-cts, since it gives the surface an ideal ase for working with glazes. With atte acrylic paint it's harder to spread ut glazes evenly because the surface is o absorbent; the end result may be ery uneven and difficult to adjust.

These finishes are applied to large reas to vary their texture, hide defects, r create decorative effects such as col-mns and arches.

Water techniques, even though they ay be very elaborate, are ideal for cre-ing smooth and rustic appearances, ith a feel of the countryside; they can so be used on objects and furniture to iggest old walls in ancient styles char-cterized by matte but attractive finishes id a very appealing freshness.

They can also be used on fairly large furniture and on small objects and acces-sories, plus lamp bases, chairs, boxes, and so forth.

The variety of surfaces is not a prob-lem as long as they are prepared prop-erly—clean, dry, and primed with an appropriate base coat; steel, plastic, wood, brass, and other materials are all suited to decorating. Although water techniques can be protected with var-nish, they're not the best choice for ex-terior applications, since they're not as durable as oil paints and finishes.

Carved wooden bird and fish decorated using water techniques.

Natural wood stains

Wood staining is a simple technique that provides very attractive results. You can create truly artistic finishes in a variety of shades. With its use of natural or earth pigments, the following technique harks back to a time before paints and stains were available commercially.

1- In a deep plastic container, prepare a glaze by mixing one part pigment of the chosen color, one-half part latex, and five parts water

2- Use medium-grit sandpaper to prepare the surface to be stained, working gently and following the grain of the wood. If there are any traces of old varnish, you'll have to sand them or strip them. You'll also have to use sandpaper or a hobbyist's knife to get rid of any glue around joints; otherwise, the glue will interfere with the staining.

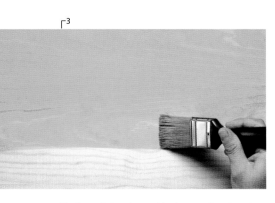

3- Spread the glaze with the wood grain using a medium sash brush so that the entire surface absorbs the stain.

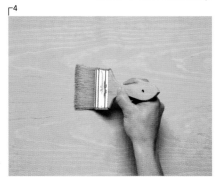

4- Next, use a chip brush to smooth out the previously applied glaze, always working in the direction of the wood grain, to assure that the glaze penetrates evenly into the wood. This operation should be done quickly so that the wood isn't exposed to too much moisture longer than necessary. If you're working with veneered wood, the veneer could come unglued through the increased moisture; that's not an issue when working with solid wood furniture.

5- Remove excess moisture with a cotton rag or paper towel until the wood is dry. Follow the wood grain to avoid streaking.
If the glaze is very thick, it can be softened by passing a damp sponge over the whole surface before it dries.

Sample of stain using magenta earth pigment.

Sample of stain using royal yellow earth pigment.

6- Once the surface is entirely dry, the color can be deepened by applying another coat of stain and repeating the preceding process. You can keep applying coats of stain until you get the shade you want; just be sure to let the surface dry thoroughly between coats.
Once the work is dry, protect it with two coats of flat oil-based varnish, allowing adequate drying time between coats.

7- Sample of stain using orange-colored earth pigment.

Worn terra-cotta

By applying various techniques of decorative painting, we can easily give objects made from any substance the appearance of a totally different material. The effect of aged and weathered terra-cotta is one of the easiest ones to create, and it's very decorative. This technique can be applied on any type of surface, and it produces a very harmonious finish.

1- With a medium-size bristle sash brush, apply a coat of acrylic primer-sealer over the entire plaster piece. Let dry; drying time is indicated on the label of the container.

2- Using a small-size bristle sash brush, apply the terra-cotta-color acrylic paint to cover the entire surface and set it aside to dry. If necessary, apply a second coat so that the surface is covered thoroughly. Let dry four hours.

3- In a container, prepare a mixture of white pigment, Spanish white, and water to make a creamy texture.
Using a small brush, apply this to the entire object, particularly to the bas relief. Let dry one hour.
The consistency of this mixture is like a paint, but since it has no binder, it can be removed from certain areas.

This type of finish must always be protected with varnish. In this case we have used a flat acrylic varnish. Very decorative effects can be created by varying the base color—for example a medium blue instead of terra-cotta color, or a light or pinkish green.

4- Use a cotton cloth moistened with water to remove part of the white on relief areas, leaving the terra-cotta color more visible on some of the high spots.

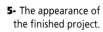

5- The appearance of the finished project.

Sponging

Sponging can provide a more or less mottled effect depending on the type of sponge used. This technique is used for decorating large areas and, with more subtle effects, on smaller objects as well. In the latter case, the choice of brighter or more subdued colors creates effects that range from discreet to spectacular.

Negative sponging

The different mottling effects created by sponging can vary according to the method and the type of sponge used to apply the paint. There are many types of sponge, both natural and artificial, that can be bought commercially and with which you can create an endless variety of effects.

3- Using a sponge moistened in water, press over the entire surface to create a negative effect and point up the background color. It's a good idea to let the paint that's treated by the sponge dry, and to change the position of the sponge to create a more pleasing effect. It's advisable to apply two or three coats of flat oil-based varnish once the paint is dry.

1- Before starting with the sponge, apply a coat of satin-finish acrylic paint to the area to be decorated; this will be easy to work with, and it will produce a more natural result. Using a sash brush to prepare the surface, spread the acrylic paint diluted with water in all directions. The solution consists of one part paint to three parts water. On large surfaces, work in sections about 1½ feet (½ m) square; otherwise the paint will dry before you can finish creating the desired effect.

2- Next, use a chip brush to spread out the paint more uniformly.

Sample of ultramarine blue with a little ochre on a light blue background.

Sample of Prussian blue with ochre on a cream colored background.

Positive sponging

Just as with negative sponge patterns, positive sponging can yield a great variety of effects depending on the type of sponge used. Positive sponging allows mixing different colors by coats to vary the finish.

1- Using a moist natural sponge, take up a small amount of paint and blot it on a plate or tray to spread the paint uniformly through the entire sponge.

2- Press the sponge lightly over the entire surface prepared in advance, moving and turning the sponge in different ways. That way it leaves a different type of track. Once the entire area has been covered with the first color, allow it to dry.

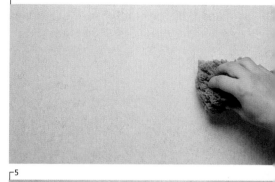

3- Repeat the same operation with a different color sponged onto the same surface. The second application softens the first and evens out the appearance. You can use the same color as in the first coat, but be careful not to cover too thoroughly or the effect will be lost.

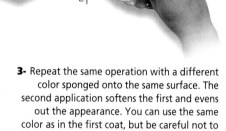

4- Finally, apply an oil-based varnish. Depending on the effect you want to create, you can use either flat or satin.

5- The finished effect using a natural sponge with natural sienna and yellow ochre on an unpainted background.

Sample done with a synthetic sponge, blue and ochre on a beige background. If several types of sponge are used on the same job, the result is richer and more elaborate effects. Also, different effects done with various types of sponge can be applied one on top of another on the same piece.

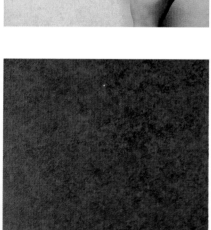

Sample of burnt sienna, Prussian blue, and carmine on a scarlet background.

Sample of orange, natural sienna, stone gray, and Prussian blue on a yellow ochre background.

Sample using natural sienna, stone gray, and dark gray on an unpainted background.

Stripping

Stripping is a technique commonly used in decoration, especially on furniture and other wooden objects. The appearance of wear and the layering of different colors make the pieces look like they're genuinely old.

This technique is not used exclusively for aging objects. You can also use layers of bright and cheerful colors to create a very contemporary and modern look.

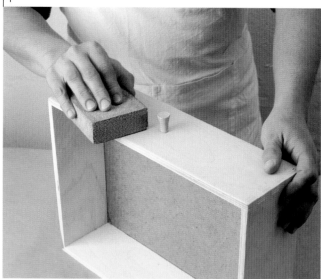

1- If the piece to be decorated is new, lightly sand the entire surface with medium-grit sandpaper. If, on the other hand, you intend to decorate a piece that's already painted, first wash the entire surface with hot water and ammonia to get rid of any dirt before sanding.

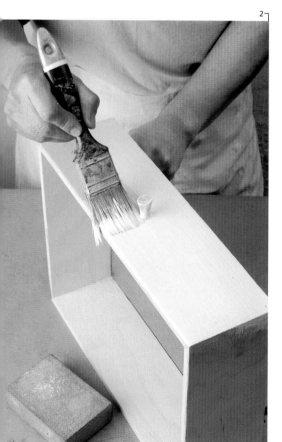

2- Apply an even coat of acrylic primer-sealer with a sash brush, taking care not to use too much on the sides; otherwise the drawers might not fit properly afterwards.
Allow to dry.
It's important to keep in mind the dimensions of the doors and drawers after applying the sealer and paint.
An excessively thick coat might keep them from closing properly when the project is done.

3- Use a medium-size brush to spread brown acrylic paint evenly over the entire piece.
If a single coat doesn't cover thoroughly, apply a second coat after the first one has dried.
After that, let dry for 24 hours.
The drying time for each paint depends on the manufacturer, so it's a good idea to read the instructions for each paint chosen for the project.

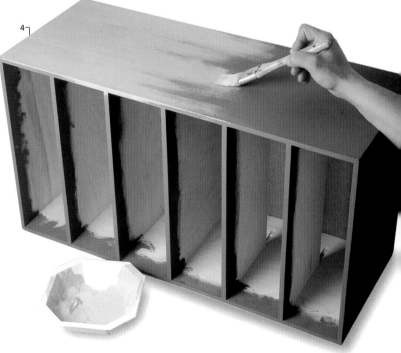

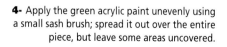

4- Apply the green acrylic paint unevenly using a small sash brush; spread it out over the entire piece, but leave some areas uncovered.

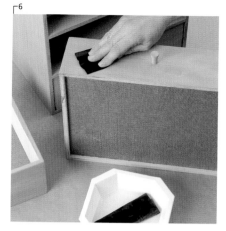

5- Next, mix some green and white paint to make a lighter shade, and paint the areas that weren't previously touched up. Let dry two hours.

6- Soak some 600-grit wet-or-dry sandpaper in water for a few minutes. Work the moistened paper unevenly over the entire surface of the piece, paying particular attention to the corners and the edges to give them the desired background color. The intensity, or the wear produced to a greater or lesser degree with the wet-or-dry sandpaper, is a function of each individual's taste, or of the type of piece that's being decorated.

7- Before the piece dries, use a cotton rag to remove the paint you've sanded. This produces a finish that's very smooth to the touch. Next, let the project dry thoroughly.

8- To finish up, varnish the whole piece with oil-based varnish applied with a sash brush. This will protect the piece from scratches. Let dry 24 hours and apply a second coat of varnish. Varnished pieces sometimes look like they've been coated with plastic. To create a much more natural-looking finish, you can dilute the varnish with turpentine in these proportions: 75% varnish to 25% turpentine.

9- Appearance of the finished project.

Roman style

The appearance of the frescos and decorated walls of the homes in ancient Rome has always been considered especially attractive. It gives a wall or an object the appearance of marble and presents a pleasing visual impression of fullness. This is created by applying superimposed transparent layers of glaze. By changing the colors used, you can create a great variety of effects.

1- The glazes are prepared by mixing in the following proportions:
1 part pigment of the desired color
½ part latex (PVA)
4 parts water
Using a sash brush, quickly apply the glaze of the desired color to a surface previously painted with satin-finish acrylic paint.
On large areas such as walls, work in areas about 3 feet (1 m) on a side, but always in undefined shapes and never in symmetrical patterns.

2- Use a chip brush to spread out the glaze. This should be done immediately, since water-based glaze dries quickly.

3- Before the glaze dries, use a cotton rag to blot and gently rub the entire area where the glaze was applied, so that the marks left by the cloth create the desired effect. For a more natural appearance, keep the marks left by the rag uneven by working in all directions: up and down, diagonally, and so forth.

4- If the final result is too pronounced, use a blender to soften the effect. Use a gentle figure-eight and up-and-down motion. Just brush the surface to create a very subtle blending.

5- On large surfaces it's a good idea to apply two coats of glaze to produce more even finishes.
Before applying a second coat, the first one must be dry. Wait at least two hours; otherwise you might damage the first coat.
Once you have achieved the desired effect and the glazes are completely dry, apply a coat of flat varnish.

Sample showing a first coat of natural sienna glaze and a second coat of ultramarine blue glaze on a yellow ochre background.

Sample showing two coats of ultramarine blue glaze with a little black on a light blue background.

Sample showing two coats of red oxide glaze with red ochre on a salmon background.

Marbling with water paints

Painters have always been interested in imitating materials that are found in nature. For centuries people have been creating decorative effects inspired by stone and marble on furniture and walls. You can create beautiful marbling using techniques with water paints and transparent glazes.

1- Working on a surface previously prepared with two coats of white satin-finish acrylic paint, use a sash brush to spread light green paint diluted with water in the proportion of one part paint to three parts water.

2- Before it dries, use a cotton cloth to create uneven, cloudy patterns, letting the background show through in some places.

3- Use a badger brush to smooth out the effects and create more depth; keep the patterns uneven. Next, let dry for a few minutes.

4- Use the sash brush to cover more areas with medium green; repeat the preceding process to blend in with the first area. Get some paint onto areas already painted to integrate the two shades of green.

5- Rub with the cotton cloth to create cloudy patterns of varying intensity; keep the effects varied.

6- Before the paint dries, use the badger brush to smooth and blend the effects. To blend the patterns and create an impression of depth, move the brush in figure eights, holding it perpendicular to the surface without pressing down. Then let dry.

7- Moisten a synthetic sponge using a sash brush dipped in medium green paint and apply it to the surface so that there are no lumps.

8- Press the sponge on some areas to leave an impression of its texture and simulate small stones. Let dry a few minutes. It's important to let each special effect dry before painting over it; if it's not dry, the previous coat may mix with the new one and be obliterated by it. Since we're working with water-based paints, drying time is relatively short.

9- Using a sash brush, go back over certain areas with light green paint; you should be able to see through it to the layer below.

10- Next, use a rag to go over the work and smooth out visible brush marks.

12- Use the badger brush very softly and without pressing down to finish blending in the sponge patterns. This brush is used gently to blend certain effects; otherwise, it may obliterate the effect you've created.

11- Before the surface dries, use a clean sponge to press on the wet paint and leave fairly dense marks.

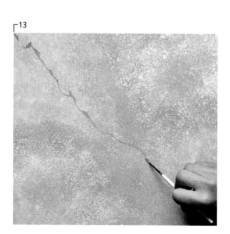

14- Before the veining dries, use the badger brush to blend it in and integrate it into the background.

13- Use a fine pencil brush and undiluted medium green paint to draw the fine veins in varying intensities and widths.

15- Press a synthetic sponge soaked in white paint onto several areas to create the impression of stones; it can also be pressed onto some of the veins to integrate them more.

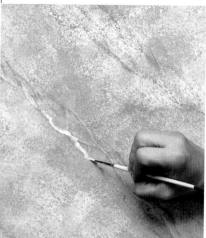

16- Accentuate certain parts of the veining by using a pencil brush to apply some white paint; this simulates the crystallization of the veins. Use the white paint only on the parts of the veins you want to highlight.

17- Move the badger brush in an upward direction to blend in the parts painted white and integrate them into the entire scheme.

18- If the veins are still too prominent, use the synthetic sponge and the medium green paint to attenuate a few sections and create a more natural appearance.

19- Use the fine pencil brush and medium green paint to apply some choppy lines and highlight the intersections between veins. Let dry.

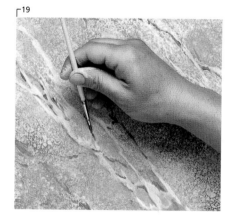

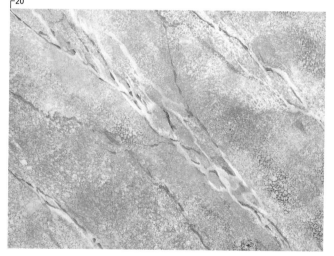

20- Finally, apply some oil-based satin-finish varnish. Here's the final appearance of the marble.

Sample of salmon and medium blue-gray on a clear ochre background.

Sample of light blue and burnt sienna on a white background.

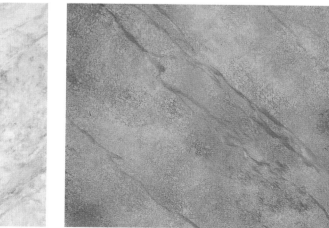

Faded texturing

It's very rewarding to work with textures and stenciling techniques because you can achieve an infinity of effects and finishes. Texturing with plaster or spackling compound can create many types of decoration, especially rustic ones, when the walls are rough or in bad condition. But this finish is not limited to walls in poor condition, since it also lends charm to other walls that show their age.

1- Prepare a very diluted red ochre glaze using one part latex, one-half part pigment, and six parts water. Use a sash brush to color the entire surface unevenly. Then let dry for two hours.

2- Prepare a batch of fairly thick plaster according to the manufacturer's directions and spread it on in all directions with a metal putty knife, dragging the plaster all around with the putty knife and leaving some spots bare. Let dry 24 hours. It's a good idea to use a drop cloth to protect the floor where you're working, because if you haven't had much experience with this you might leave some stains.

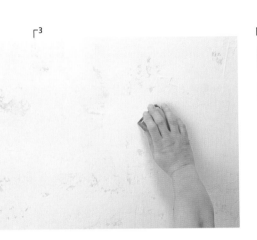

3- If you have left some unsightly spots in the plaster, sand them with coarse sandpaper to conceal them; but don't press too hard, and proceed with care because the abrasive can leave marks.

4- For the appearance of wear to be more attractive, you must leave some spots with no plaster; this will provide a fairly subtle contrast with the color applied afterward.

5- Prepare a glaze using yellow ochre, mixing one part latex, one part pigment, and four parts water. Next, dip a cotton rag in the glaze. Wring it out a little so it doesn't drip too much, and color the entire plastered surface by rubbing it in circular motions. Let dry 24 hours.

6- If you want a dark color, repeat the same operation with the ochre. You can also obtain some very attractive effects by repeating this step with a different color to create different shades using transparent layers.

7- Choose the design you want to stencil and trace it with a permanent marker on a sheet of acetate.

8- Use a hobbyist's knife or a scalpel to cut out the selected design. To protect your work surface, place the acetate onto a polyester backing.

9- Paint the selected design using a stenciling brush. Be gentle and subtle; the figure should appear natural and not touched up.

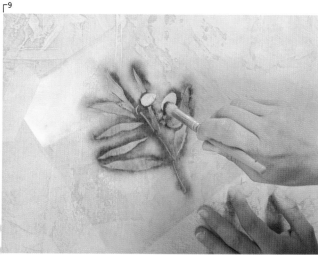

10- To integrate the design into the background, sand it unevenly to simulate wear due to the passage of time. It wouldn't look right if the wall appeared old and the stenciling looked as if it were brand new.

11- The finished wall.

Wear and tear

There are many ways of giving objects an appearance of wear by rubbing them to beautify or accentuate the color.

A representative example follows. This is a very simple way to decorate objects and furniture and give them a very special finish.

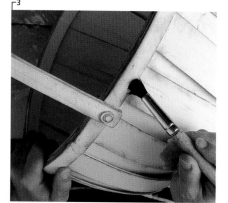

1- After lightly sanding the entire surface, apply bone-color acrylic paint using a medium sash brush. If the color doesn't cover completely, let it dry and apply a second coat. In this example we have chosen a new basket made of untreated wood. If you want to decorate an object or piece of furniture that's already been painted, apply a coat of acrylic primer-sealer before painting.

2- When the paint is dry, sand the edges and corners, removing the paint in certain places, so that they look worn. After sanding, remove all dust from the object so the paint will stick properly.

3- Take up a little bit of hazelnut-colored paint using a stiff pencil brush, blotting the excess on a paper towel. Shade the corners and high places with varying amounts of color, emphasizing certain places over others. For this exercise we have chosen very natural colors such as bone and hazelnut, but you can create some very appealing effects with bolder colors such as yellow with green, orange with purple, turquoise with purple, and so forth. It's a good idea to do some color test pieces as you try to come up with different combinations.

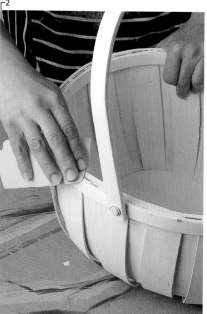

4- When the paint is dry, apply a flat or satin-finish aerosol varnish if you want a little sheen. You can also use other types of varnish for the finish, such as acrylic or oil-based ones.

5- The appearance of the finished article.

Faded plaster

The deteriorated appearance of faded, damaged, and porous plaster can be applied to many decors, whether rustic or old and modern. Transparent layers created by applying colors in varying dilutions create a very special appearance of depth. This technique is easy and very suitable for large surfaces, since its effect is more obvious on them than on small objects.

1- Prepare a mixture of three parts water, one part pigment, and one part latex; also add 2 tablespoons of Spanish white to give the mixture some texture.
On a surface previously prepared with flat acrylic paint, use a bristle sash brush to cover the entire area a little at a time, letting the diluted paint run. Leave some streaks so the color doesn't turn out too even. Let dry five hours.

2- After the paint is dry, use a clean brush soaked in water to dampen the area in sections about 3 feet (1 m) square; this operation will make the next one easier.

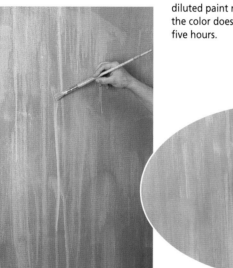

To lighten the shade and dilute the mixture a little more, add a little white pigment to it, mixing one part paint to two of water. With a small pencil brush, apply some of the new color in a pattern of uneven stripes; the brush will have to be well loaded so that the paint sometimes runs in gobs.

Using a natural sponge moistened with water, wet and smudge the stripes and the lines formed by the large drops of paint. Work in sections, pressing the sponge on the patterns for a few seconds and repeating the operation so that the sponge pattern becomes visible.

To eliminate effects that are too obvious, use a chip brush to blend in the biggest drops of paint, moving the brush upward. You can create some very distinct effects by combining colors other than the ones used in this illustration. With different shades of gray, faded plaster will look like lead, and with neutral and burnt siennas it will look very luminous and cozy.

6- Appearance of the finished project. The decorated surface can be protected with flat acrylic varnish so it's more durable.

Texturing

The different textures and the relief presented by some surfaces can often work to your advantage in creating various finishes. In other instances, new walls that are too smooth can be treated to give them a subtle surface texture and make for some attractive decorative effects.

The following operation is a simple example of how to use paint to create a textured decorative effect.

1- Apply some very thick, light gray satin-finish acrylic paint using short brush strokes in all directions in such a way that you leave visible marks from the bristles. When you press on the brush, you leave small furrows and create a subtle texture graven into the surface. Let dry two hours. If the brush strokes are not very noticeable, you'll have to wait until the paint starts to dry a little and repeat the operation with a dry brush to accentuate the texture. Work in areas about 3 feet (1 m) square to keep the texture fairly regular.

2- Prepare a glaze using ultramarine blue, ochre, white, and a little black in these proportions: one part latex, one part pigment and four parts water.
Use a brush to slap it on in all directions, continuing to work in areas about 3 feet square. It's important to spread the paint unevenly to avoid leaving stripes with vertical or horizontal shapes.

3- Before the glaze dries, use a dry broad brush to spread out the glaze in all directions so that it penetrates well into the little furrows left by the bristles in the previous operation.

4- When the glaze starts to dry, continue brushing in all directions with a very dry broad brush; this gently spreads the glaze on the high points. Let dry two hours.

5- To augment the appearance of wear, lightly brush the surface with a stiff scrub brush. This step is optional and may be omitted if you don't want to exaggerate the effect.

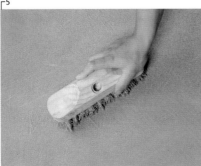

6- Mark a line at a little over 3 feet (1 m) from the floor to indicate the height of the chair rail and apply masking tape to cover it. Use the same glaze to repeat the first step, once again spreading it in all directions. Accentuate the color with a second coat so that the part with the chair rail is darker. This second coat can be done with a different color than the first one to create greater contrast. If you use contrasting colors, you can make the part under the chair rail appear different from the rest of the wall. You can also use several colors to create very decorative effects of depth as they are applied in transparent layers.

Use a chip brush to spread the glaze out in all directions, evening out the color and eliminating streaks of different shades. Dry the brush frequently with a rag to remove the glaze it accumulates, and keep it as dry as possible as you work.

8- To stain the natural wood molding, prepare a mixture of ultramarine blue acrylic paint with a little black added, and dilute it with water to make it more liquid, in the proportions of one part paint to one part water. Spread it out evenly over the entire surface to color the wood. Let dry 24 hours.

9- Prepare a diluted flat acrylic paint by mixing one part paint to two parts water and spread it over the surface of the wood, working in about 4-foot (1.5-m) sections.

10- Before the paint dries, use a rag moistened with water to rub the wood unevenly in sections to let some patches of the first color show through. If the paint has dried too much, rub it gently with a rag moistened with methyl alcohol.

11- Use flat acrylic varnish to coat the wood and protect it. If you want a brighter finish, you can use satin-finish varnish.
If you want to protect the entire wall from scratches and dust, use a roller to varnish the whole area that's been decorated.

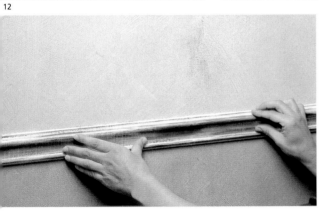

12- Use contact cement to glue the chair rail to the wall, using as a reference point the line previously drawn at the appropriate height. If the panels of the molding are large enough, use a few finishing nails to hold it more securely. To mask the nail heads, carefully putty them over and touch them up with paint.

13- Appearance of the finished project

Crackling with water paints

Crazed or crackled finishes are among the most effective ones that can be applied for aging and simulating the passage of time on furniture and other pieces. This type of decoration originated in France in the eighteenth century. There are various formulas to create this finish, but they're not always easy to carry to completion. That's why we've chosen to illustrate this water technique, which is the easiest one to use.

1- Apply a thin coat of acrylic primer-sealer to the plaster object. Let dry three hours. Use masking tape to cover the areas you don't intend to decorate with crackle glaze.

2- Thoroughly apply a coat of garnet-colored paint using a synthetic-bristle sash brush and allow to dry.
If necessary, apply a second coat to give a uniform color. Let dry between two and three hours.
The color you choose to paint the base is the one that later will be visible in the crevices of the crackled finish.

3- Paint the base of the piece with English green to create a contrast with the top part. Let dry, and if necessary, apply a second coat of the same color. Let dry two to three hours.

4- Next, apply as evenly as possible, using vertical strokes, a coat of transparent acrylic crackling varnish to the top of the piece; use a synthetic-bristle sash brush for this operation. The thicker the coat of varnish, the greater the crackling effect. Let dry one hour. Drying time also depends on ambient temperature; if the area is very dry, you may need to wait only a half-hour. The thinner and finer the coat of crackling varnish, the smaller and more numerous the cracks.

5- Next, spread a thin coat of crackling varnish using horizontal brush strokes over the lower part so that there are horizontal furrows that contrast with the top. Let dry one hour.

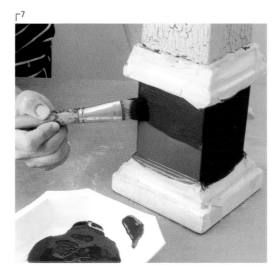

7- Next, apply the garnet paint as evenly as possible to the base of the piece, using horizontal brush strokes. Once the paint has started to dry, some horizontal cracks will appear and you will be able to see some of the background color.

8- Paint the rest of the piece with English red. Let it dry for two hours.

6- Using a soft bristle brush dipped in cream-colored paint, apply an even coat to the garnet-colored surface. When the paint dries, the cracks will start to appear. Let dry two hours.
Spread enough paint to cover the entire area with a single coat, for if you have to touch it up, the surface may not crack as it should. If you want to speed up the appearance of the cracks, you can use a hair dryer or put the piece under a heat lamp; the heat will speed up the process.

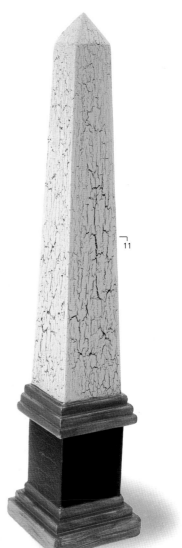

▪ Next, using a sash brush with synthetic ▪ristles, brush the gold color onto the surface ▪eviously painted with English red, leaving ▪me areas only partially covered. Let dry ▪e hour.

▪- If you want to accentuate the streaking, or ▪ the gold is too opaque, use a sash brush to ▪ply a little English red over the gold to make ▪ look worn. Let dry.

11- To improve the durability of this finish, apply a coat of flat oil-based varnish. If the crackled finish is applied to a piece of furniture, it's a good idea to use two or three coats of varnish, allowing 24 hours' drying time between coats.

Dragged decoupage

Several techniques are used in this procedure. It's an example of the great variety of effects that can be achieved by using different combinations of finishes. Brushwork was used as a variation of glazing techniques, particularly in the eighteenth century. You apply a transparent paint to a smooth surface and drag a brush over it to reveal small, fine lines of the base color.

1- On a surface previously painted with satin-finish acrylic paint, spread a coat of acrylic yellow ochre paint diluted with two parts water to one part paint. Work in areas about 3 feet (1 m) square.

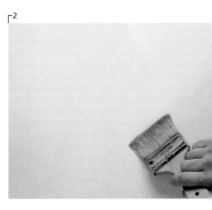

2- Before the paint dries, use a chip brush to spread the paint out thin, brushing it in all directions to create an effect of depth. Keep brushing it out until you can see some of the color underneath.

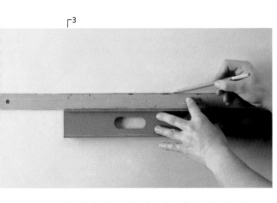

3- To indicate the height of the dividing line, measure up from the floor and use a level and a ruler to mark a horizontal line. Measure the vertical lines in the same way; in this case they are about 6 inches (15 cm) wide.

4- Use masking tape to protect the outside edges of the stripes and make it easier to keep them straight. It's a good idea to use tape to mark the sections you don't want to paint so you don't make a mistake.
When you're painting stripes on baseboards or walls, it's easy to make a mistake and paint the wrong space, and any kind of mark or sign will help you avoid that. Before you start painting the stripes, check them over one by one to be sure you've taped the sections properly.

5- Acrylic paints are water-based, and they dry quickly. In order to have more time to create the desired effects, you may want to buy an additive that slows down the drying time, such as acrylic drying retardant. Thoroughly mix equal portions of ultramarine blue acrylic paint and the drying retardant. Use this mixture to paint the vertical stripes, taking care to cover completely.

6- Use a thoroughly dry chip brush and press gently with a downward motion, leaving a slight brush mark. The striping comes out best if it's done at a single pass. Dry the brush well every time you use it on a stripe; you'll need to eliminate the excess paint it picks up. Let dry 24 hours.

7- The same way you marked the vertical stripes, mark off a horizontal line about 1½ inches (3.5 cm) wide and paint it as indicated. Use a perfectly dry synthetic-bristle sash brush moved horizontally to create the same type of subtle striping that you created in the wide stripes. Let dry 24 hours.

8- The design chosen for decorating with this technique can be an original one, such as these fish, or you can look for designs in magazines, books, and other places, and enlarge or shrink them on a photocopier to adapt them to the space where they will be used. Apply the color to the photocopies; the acrylic paint will have to be very dilute so they'll look like they were painted with watercolors.
This subtle way of coloring the photocopied illustrations makes them look more handmade.

9- With a hobby knife or scissors, cut out the illustrations to be used for decorating the walls. Decorating with paper cutouts is a long historical tradition. It was used especially at the end of the eighteenth century, when engravings were cut out to glue onto walls, furniture, and other pieces.
Nowadays, the photocopy machine allows us to use an endless number of designs, repeating and integrating them in many decorations.

10- Apply a fine layer of repositionable aerosol adhesive to the back of the designs. This type of glue allows you to distribute the designs on the surface and move them around until you get the layout you want.

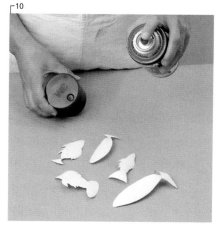

11- Your hands should be perfectly clean as you stick the small fish onto the wall in the desired pattern. The figures have been distributed in a random pattern, but they could be applied differently, as in a horizontal border, or in horizontal rows in the spaces between stripes. Whatever pattern you choose, this will make for an attractive decoration.

12- Apply a coat of flat acrylic varnish over the entire surface to protect the photocopies applied to the wall. On large areas it's a good idea to use a foam roller to keep the varnish even. Let dry six hours and apply a second coat of varnish.
If decoupage decoration is used on a table or other piece that's subject to lots of wear, it's important to protect it with several coats of varnish, up to five or six, to make sure that the decoration won't get scratched.

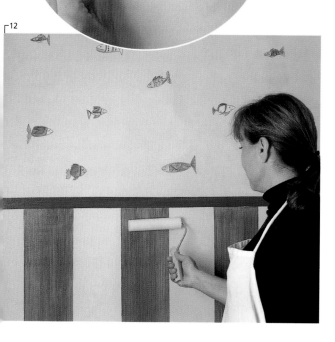

13- Appearance of the finished project

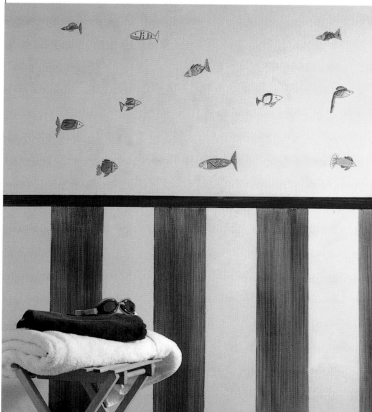

Imitation stone

Imitating different types of stones and marbles with different painting techniques has been done for a long time in decorative painting. Specifically, decorative painters of past centuries used imitation stone techniques to decorate staircase landings, columns, and small objects.

1- Sand the entire surface of the Styrofoam form to smooth the uneven spots that characterize it—especially any mold marks.

2- Next, apply a base coat of acrylic primer-sealer to the entire surface, filling the small holes in the material. Let dry one hour. For ease in holding the object, stick it onto the handle of a pencil brush and hold it by the handle.

3- With a bristle brush and slightly diluted burnt umber paint, cover the whole surface of the sphere unevenly.

4- Before the acrylic paint dries, use the brush to poke the surface lightly and create a slightly more uniform stippled effect and to eliminate any remaining brush strokes. Let dry ten minutes.

5- Use a natural sponge and burnt umber to apply a light coat of paint, leaving some lighter-colored areas. Let dry ten minutes.

6- To create the appearance of small veins, paint some small, uneven lines over the whole surface with a fan brush and some white paint. Let dry ten minutes.

7- Cut out some small pieces of newspaper in various shapes and sizes and put them into a container.

8- Pour some water into the container to moisten the cutout pieces of paper.

9- Arrange the various pieces of paper over the entire surface of the sphere, mixing sizes and shapes and pressing them on so that they stay.

10- Using a natural sponge, quickly cover the surface with English red so that the texture of the sponge is visible.

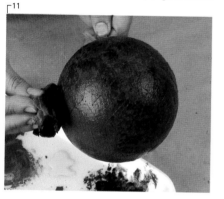

11- Before it's entirely dry, repeat the process with burnt umber; since the paint is still wet, the two colors will mix.

12- Use the sponge to apply a coat of light pink, covering as thoroughly as possible and mixing it with the previous color; this produces a surface with different shades.

13- Repeat the process with some English red mixed with a little terra-cotta color, but this time use a lighter coat to avoid obscuring the previous colors.

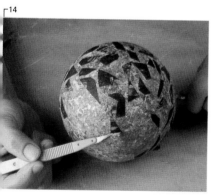

14- Before the paint dries completely, use the point of a hobby knife or some scissors to carefully remove the pieces of newspaper. Then the different textures that simulate small stones will appear. Apply three coats of glossy acrylic varnish. If you want a more rustic stone finish, use flat varnish.

15- Appearance of the finished project.

Chipping

Superimposing different colors and shades can create visual effects of great beauty. This type of finish gives objects and furniture a gentle beauty, especially in rustic decors, that naturally occurs with the passage of time.

1- This plain but attractive lamp base, made of unpainted wood, is ideally suited to this type of finish. Lightly sand the entire surface using medium-grit sandpaper.

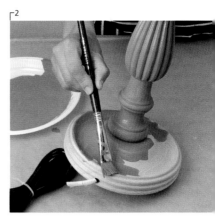

2- In a container, make a diluted solution of three parts medium brown paint and one part water to make a more fluid consistency. Use a synthetic-bristle brush to cover the entire surface of the piece and let dry one hour. This first step stains the wood a darker color; you can also combine bolder base colors, such as red or lemon green.

3- To protect the paint, apply a coat of flat oil-based varnish diluted with oil of turpentine in the ratio of 70% varnish to 30% oil of turpentine. Spread this evenly over the entire surface and let dry 24 hours.

4- Apply a coat of white acrylic paint to the entire surface, paying particular attention to the raised areas. Let dry two hours.

5- Using medium-grit sandpaper, lightly sand the entire surface, rubbing harder on the raised parts and uncovering small sections of the first color that look like scratches and simulate damage.

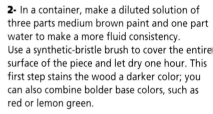

6- To create the appearance of minor chipping, rub various sections with fine steel wool to reveal some of the base coat. Clean the piece of all traces of dust and sanding.

7- To give the surface a smooth and satiny finish, apply a coat of colorless furniture wax to the entire surface using a cotton rag; let dry a half-hour.
The wax gives the piece a pleasing feel and an old-looking finish. You can also use colored waxes to create a more noticeable effect.
Use a chamois cloth to buff the piece and give it the satiny appearance that old objects have.

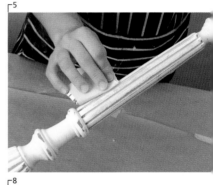

8- By complementing this lamp base with a shade decorated using the same technique, you end up with a piece that is adaptable to many different decors. Even though this is a somewhat coarse and rustic finish, it can lend an air of sophistication to some areas.

Dragging and texturing

Superimposing different diluted colors produces excellent results in decorating furniture and objects; it's also very decorative on doors and windows. This is a simple technique, but it has to be done quickly for the best dragging effect.

1- Apply a coat of yellow ochre satin-finish acrylic paint to the surface of the piece previously prepared with acrylic sealer. The paint needs to be thick, since you will press it on with the brush to give it a striated texture in one direction.
The effect will be more decorative if the texture that you create in this step is boldly striated. Let dry two hours.

2- Dilute some light brown flat acrylic paint by mixing one part paint and one part water; apply in sections using a medium natural-bristle sash brush. Sometimes you can use a brush that's been used a lot and is stiff; it will leave striated brush strokes as you spread the paint.

3- Before the paint dries, drag a dry chip brush over the area to spread the paint out well in the grooves in the textured base coat. Let dry one hour.

4- Using medium-grit sandpaper, lightly sand the piece unevenly to make the surface look old and expose part of the base color. Then remove any sanding dust.

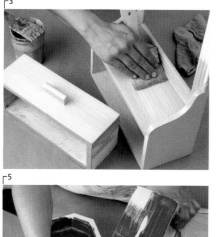

5- Prepare the indigo blue in a container by mixing one part pigment, three parts water, and one part latex; the result is a fairly dilute paint. Spread the paint on evenly in sections.

6- Before the paint dries, brush it with a thoroughly dry chip brush to reveal the various colors and shades underneath. To protect the work, you next apply a flat oil-based varnish. You have to use a completely dry brush for this part of the operation, so you'll need to dry it with rags or paper towels and remove the paint it picks up.

7- Appearance of the finished project

Oxidizing with iron sulfate

Oxidized finishes on decorative objects, metal furniture, and lamp bases are very common nowadays. One of the most interesting aspects of oxidizing with iron sulfate is that it can be applied to any surface (plastic, wood, plaster, and others) that's been prepared properly, to create the appearance of metal.

1- Mix acrylic paint with water to make a more liquid paint, using one part paint to six parts water. The result should be like tinted water. Use this color to spread an uneven coat over the entire piece without covering it entirely.

2- Repeat the preceding step using natural sienna, paying particular attention to the raised areas and nooks and crannies.
The piece that's being decorated here is a section of plaster molding that has not been treated with any kind of primer. If you want to create this same effect on another type of material, such as plastic, styrofoam, or wood, apply one or two coats of acrylic primer-sealer.

3- Cover the entire piece with red oxide similarly diluted with water; let the previous colors show through in certain spots.

4- Use a dark brown to paint the high spots without completely covering the previous colors.
The warm colors that have been chosen are suited to creating the final effect, but they can be varied to create a more artistic oxide.

5- Repeat the process with the same dark brown color to darken the shade in certain areas. Then let dry. Even if you choose different color shades for the base coat, it's a good idea that some of them be dark; that will highlight the oxide more effectively.

6- Prepare the iron sulfate by dissolving it in water. Moisten the entire piece with liberal amounts of this solution. Let dry in a well-ventilated area.
If you want to achieve a very oxidized appearance, apply more liquid as the piece begins to dry.
It's a good idea to use latex gloves since iron sulfate is a very strong oxidizer. You should also protect the work surface.
To speed up the oxidation process, leave the piece in a well-ventilated place. The time required for oxidizing depends on the climate and the degree of oxidation desired.

8- If the piece is oxidized evenly all over, you can accentuate certain high points by using a nearly dry brush to apply some liquid asphaltum to various places. This will provide more contrast in the appearance of the piece.

9- Use paper towels to remove excess asphaltum from various places.

7- The right amount of oxidation is up to each individual to determine. The longer the piece is allowed to oxidize, the greater the effect of the iron oxide. Once the piece has reached the appropriate amount of oxidation, you have to apply varnish to protect it. That's how you stop the process of oxidation. It's important to do a good job of varnishing the piece; you may need to use two or three coats of flat oil-based varnish.

10- Appearance of the completed piece.

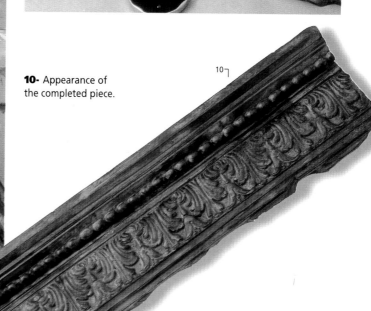

Aged scumbling

There are an infinite variety of effects that can be achieved using water techniques. Scumbling is one example. This is a very simple technique that produces a very decorative finish. It can be used on large areas as well as small pieces of furniture and other objects.

1- In a container mix one part of medium blue acrylic paint and two parts water. Next, spread the diluted medium blue acrylic paint unevenly onto a surface previously painted with light blue satin-finish acrylic paint.

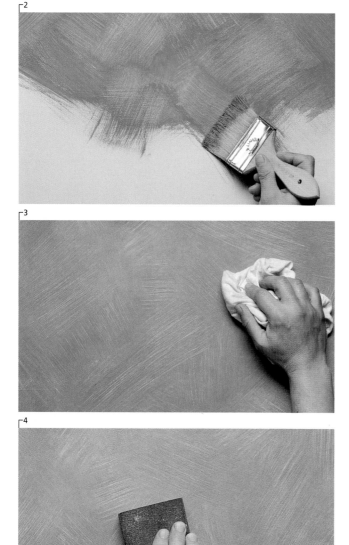

2- Use a chip brush to spread the paint out in all directions; work quickly while the paint is still wet. On large surfaces, work in sections no larger than about 3 feet (1 m) square so that you have time to spread the paint out in all directions before it dries.

3- While the paint is still wet, rub over the entire surface with a cotton rag, exposing the base color in various spots.
If the paint has dried, you can use a cotton rag moistened with water to rub the surface.

4- You can enhance the scumbling by lightly sanding the entire area with medium-grit sandpaper. This helps keep the finish even on large surfaces. This step is optional and is used in case the procedure with the rag doesn't yield the desired appearance.

5- Once the work has dried, protect it with an even coat of flat oil-based varnish applied to the entire surface.

6- This is the appearance that this technique produces. As you can see, it's very attractive, and on large surfaces it can be a spectacular finish.

7- If you prefer a finish that looks even older, you can apply a patina of asphaltum mixed with wax. Using a medium brush, spread the mixture of asphaltum and wax over the entire surface. This mixture allows you more time to work the aged finish, since the wax not only softens the effect, but also slows the drying of the asphaltum.

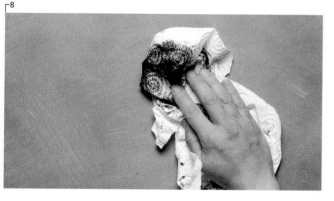

8- Before it dries, gently wipe off the excess patina with a paper towel until you get an even shade. You can also use a cotton cloth instead of paper towel. If the appearance created by the asphaltum and wax is too dark, you can lighten it by rubbing the surface with a rag and some clear furniture wax. This removes the excess patina and produces a more subdued appearance.

9- Aged finish. Sometimes scumbling can be applied to create decorative aging only on the lower 3 feet (1 m) of a wall that otherwise might be treated with wainscoting. The final result is very decorative.

Sample scumbled finish in ochre on a natural background; no special aging applied.

Sample scumbled finish in pistachio green on a yellow background; no special aging applied.

Oil techniques

Throughout the ages, people have at-
tempted to reproduce different materials and textures—sometimes out of necessity, and sometimes in a spirit
of experimentation. You can achieve any number of finishes using
oil techniques, which are the best ones for many types of finishes. These
techniques are used to reproduce the appearance of exotic woods and the richness of some types of marbles and precious stones; the results can be spectacular. With a little imagination and creativity, you can also create
modern finishes. These techniques use oil as the basic binder in
greater or lesser proportions in preparing the paints and glazes
that are applied to create very attractive effects. Since they
dry quite slowly, they afford a comparatively long time to
create the desired effects. This can also be a disadvantage, though, since you may have to wait a matter of days for the surface to dry thoroughly as
you apply various coats.

Decorating with oil techniques

Experiments using various binders with different drying times led painters and craftsmen in former times to use numerous vegetable oils to lengthen the drying time of the paint and give them more time to create different effects.

Linseed oil and walnut oil are the ones most commonly used in manufacturing these paints and glazes, since they dry after a certain amount of time. This would not be possible with olive oil, which never dries. The composition of oil paints has scarcely changed since the fifteenth century.

Applications

Once dry, oil-based finishes are very resistant, so they are used for decorative applications that are subject to more abrasion and wear. Doors and windows are often treated with oil-based paints because they are more durable and waterproof once dry. Used as base coats, enamels and alkyd paints in neutral colors are good for preparing a surface and subsequently applying special finishes with good results. These can be bought in a broad palette of colors in specialty shops. They can also be mixed with universal colorings to fine-tune the color. Their composition using synthetic resins mixed with oils makes for very durable paints for industrial applications, although they take longer to dry than water-based paints. They can be had in flat, satin, and gloss finishes, but satin-finish paints are the best choice for creating special effects.

Oil paints can be used to create a variety of effects. This decor highlights the wall in natural and beige colors and imitates moiré fabric.

Decorative effects

Many elements can be combined to create a particular atmosphere, including colors, furniture, fabrics, and others. Using the various effects that painting puts within our reach, it becomes a lot easier to create decors and atmospheres in large areas and on simple objects.

Working with oil techniques and with some basic knowledge, you can get satisfactory results even if you're not a big-time professional. The formulas for the various oil glazes have scarcely changed in recent centuries, and even though there are always new products in specialty shops, the basic mixtures are the same ones that have long been used by professional decorative painters and craftsmen. It's very gratifying to master this technique little by little as you create desired decorative effects. Moving slowly and using an appropriate number of brushes and tools in combination with

adequate surface preparation, you can become very competent at applying decorative finishes.

You generally work with the same formulas; what determines one effect or another is how you work with them, whether using rags, pieces of plastic, sponges, or different types of brushes.

Oil effects, and especially transparencies and overlays of different glazes of the same or different colors, can create different types of finishes. The texture of the oils produces very elegant decorations and sophisticated finishes; you can use them to create simple, modern effects or sumptuous marbles and the appearance of woods.

Wainscoting painted with oils imitating dark wood construction.

Where to use these techniques

These techniques can be applied to an infinite number of projects. There are some tremendous decorations on walls incorporating combinations of stones, decorated ceilings with skies, and even floors that look like marble or other materials. Baseboards, coronas, and architectural elements decorated with this technique add atmosphere and can be used to create historical or personal styles.

Just as with water techniques, oils can be applied to any type of surface—metals, wood, plaster, and others—given the right preparation, a clean and dry surface, and the right primer-sealer.

Apply two coats of oil-based satin-

finish paint to the surface you intend to decorate, allowing adequate drying time between coats. This base will allow you to work decorative effects with oils. This type of paint gives off strong fumes and it's harmful to inhale them, so it's important to work in well-ventilated areas. You'll also have to keep the room where you're decorating entirely free of dust, which could spoil the finish.

When this technique is applied to furniture and small pieces, it makes for some attractive decorative finishes. Even though this type of paint gives a more durable finish, it's a good idea to use oil-based or polyurethane varnish to protect the results so that they stand up better to the effects of wear.

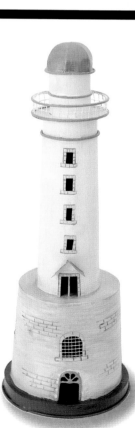

Reproduction of an antique brass toy decorated with oils.

Oil glazes

It's very easy to create decorative effects using this technique, and at the same time it can be fun to experiment with different materials and pieces to come up with different finishes. In contrast to varnish finishes, which dry quite quickly, working with oil glazes allows you to create more elaborate effects, since they take longer to dry.

Waves

A wavy effect is sometimes used in modern, vitalistic decoration of furniture and other surfaces. This is an instance where even though oil techniques are among the oldest, they can be used imaginatively to create very contemporary results.

1- Prepare a glaze by mixing one part linseed oil to two parts oil of turpentine, a few drops of universal dryer, and oil-based orange paint. Spread this glaze out on a surface previously painted with oil-based white satin-finish paint to cover the entire area you intend to decorate.

2- Using a chip brush that's completely dry, create subtle waves by pressing the brush as you drag the glaze in a downward direction. You can leave some areas with no waves to give the appearance of stripes. You can also use brushes that are a little old or stiff to make the effects more obvious.

3- Appearance of the finished project.

Checkerboard effect

The appearance of almost three-dimensional depth is easy to create using the checkerboard system. By using ochre or brown colors you can create finishes that look like braided cords of some chair seats or basket-weave designs.

1- Brush ultramarine blue glaze onto a surface previously painted with a neutral-color oil-based satin-finish paint. Next, apply an even coat of glaze using a chip brush and let stand for two minutes.

2- Using a small, dry chip brush or an old sash brush, mark off small squares in alternating directions—one vertical, the next horizontal—to create a pattern of woven squares. As some of the color accumulates on the edges of each square, you create a shading effect that looks three-dimensional.

3- Appearance of the finished project.

Using newspaper

Old newspapers are good for creating this glaze since they're so easy to obtain. You can also use other types of paper such as wrapping paper or tissue paper to create subtly different finishes.

1- Spread a carmine lacquer glaze onto a background previously painted with oil-based white satin-finish paint.

2- Use a dry chip brush to spread the glaze out in all directions and let it stand for two minutes so it begins to dry.

3- Using crumpled-up pages of newspaper, press unevenly over the entire surface, leaving impressions of the wrinkles in the paper and letting parts of the base color show through.

4- To create more dramatic effects, use a badger brush to blend and create greater transparency and a cloudy finish integrated with the background.

5- Appearance of the finished project. You can create an endless number of effects with oil glazes if you use a little imagination and the right combination of colors; the finishes can be very creative and decorative.

1- Prepare a light green glaze by mixing one part flat oil-based varnish, one-half part linseed oil, and one-half part oil of turpentine. Keep adding color to the oil until you get a transparent glaze that has the same consistency as the color. Work on surfaces that have previously been painted with satin-finish oil-based paint—white in this case.
Use a sash brush to spread the glaze over the surface in all directions. If you're decorating a piece of furniture, do first one side then the other; working in sections gives you enough time to create the special effects before the paint dries.

Glazes with varnish

Oil glazes usually are slow to dry. In order to speed up the drying process you can add appropriate amounts of varnish to the glazes.

By using glazes and the right combinations of colors you can create transparent effects and produce an endless variety of cheerful and attractive decorative finishes that can be applied in many places, such as on walls, objects, and furniture.

In the following pages we'll examine a few simple examples involving different applications; if you let your imagination have free rein, you can come up with many more types of finishes.

3- If you want a smoother base, blend the surface with the badger brush to mask and blend the brush marks from the previous step. You'll have to work quickly so the glaze doesn't start to dry.

4- In this case we have selected a rubber graining tool; these can be bought in specialty shops, and they come in different widths and shapes. Use the side of the tool that looks like a comb, and move it in a downward direction as you make repeated S-patterns. As you press down with the rubber tool, it drags the glaze and lets the base color show through, creating a type of three-dimensional pattern. You can also make out of cardboard different combs of varying sizes to create a variety of effects.

5- Here's what the finished project looks like. This finish with a serpentine effect can be applied to many types of surfaces, from boxes to wainscoting. The effect is very decorative. First you should practice the technique on a piece of wood to find out what type of design you like best.
If the glaze begins to dry too quickly, or if you make a mistake, you can erase with a rag moistened with oil of turpentine; that will get you back to the base coat, and you can start over.

2- To spread the glaze evenly, go over it with a chip brush; that will also keep if from running.

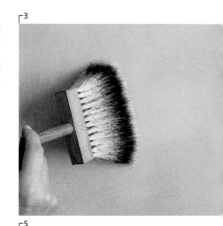

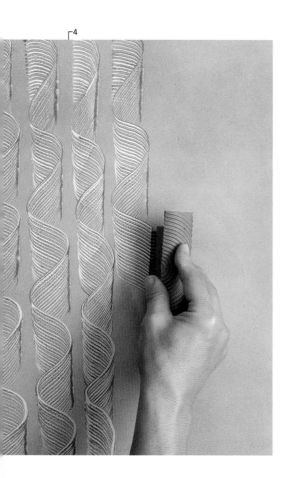

1- Prepare a glaze with magenta coloring and spread it onto a surface previously painted with oil-based white satin-finish paint.

2- Use a chip brush to even out the glaze on the surface.

3- Use the badger brush to smooth out the glaze and create an effect of greater depth; keep the brush moving vertically and in figure eights.
The brush should be used softly and held perpendicular to the surface.
Another effect that's very easy and just as attractive involves using the badger brush to smooth out the glaze in all directions. This produces a very cloudy effect.

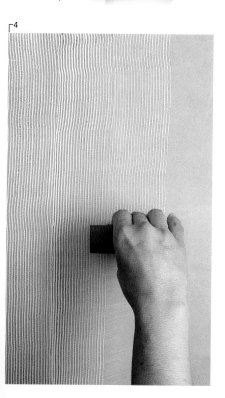

4- Move the rubber comb over the surface from top to bottom to create stripes on the surface. The stripes don't have to be perfectly straight, since it's a plus that the work was done by hand.

5- Before the glaze dries, use the comb to mark horizontal lines and create a fine cross-hatching pattern.
You can use different colors if you want to create different types of finishes working with the same process.

6- Appearance of the finished project. Using this technique you can decorate many things, from small pieces to baby or children's furniture, and give them a very special touch.

Wood glazes with varnish

With a graining pad you can also make imitation wood grain; if you choose brown shades, which are usual for woods, the finishes are very convincing.

There are different sizes of rubber tools that are used for imitating knots in wood; the one in the picture is medium-size, but there are also wider ones made for use on large surfaces.

1- Spread a dark burnt-color glaze onto a surface previously painted with oil-based yellow ochre satin-finish paint.

2- Use a chip brush to spread out the glaze smoothly over the entire surface so that the brush strokes are subdued and aligned in one direction; that determines the direction of the wood grain.

3- Hold the graining pad in your fingers and pass it over the surface from top to bottom so that it impresses its texture onto the glaze; the slower it's oscillated as it's moved downward, the larger the knot. The curved face of the cylinder has to remain in contact with the varnish, and you oscillate it so that the entire tool leaves marks at different angles as it's moved across the surface. You should try this motion on the surface of a practice piece until you get the desired effect. Use a rag to clean off the tool frequently; you'll have to remove the glaze that accumulates in the grooves. The movements must be gentle, since brusque moves leave patterns that aren't very attractive.

4- If the veining tool leaves too much glaze in certain spots, smooth the surface by moving the chip brush toward the interior of the knot to make the finish look more real.

5- Appearance of the finished project. You can use bolder colors such as blues, reds, and greens; that will give the appearance of stained wood. We have used a rubber graining pad for these effects, but you can try other objects: rags, pieces of plastic, cork pads, and any other thing that can be used to drag the glaze and leave an impression of its texture can be used in working with glazes with varnish.

The room where you work must be free of dust, which will stick to the surface of the varnish. It's a good idea to use the vacuum cleaner and wash the surface thoroughly before starting to work. That will keep the finish in perfect condition.

Whisking or flogging

There are infinite combinations that can be created with oils; whisking is one of the techniques that is used in direct imitation of wood. You can use whisking to create the look of wood finishes on doors, windows, furniture, and other small pieces. You can make even more fantastic finishes by varying the colors used.

1- Prepare a transparent glaze by mixing one part linseed oil to two parts oil of turpentine and a couple drops of universal dryer.
Use a chip brush to spread the glaze over the area you are decorating, which has previously been prepared with two coats of off-white oil-based satin-finish paint.

2- Next, use the chip brush to spread the mixture evenly over the entire surface. It's important to do this step correctly, since it determines how even the final results will be.

3- Dip a small sash brush into a little glaze and some burnt sienna oil color; apply in uneven streaks to the area being decorated. Apply the dark burnt color little by little, followed by English red, until the area being decorated has been covered completely. Paint the stripes vertically so that they all follow the same direction.

4- Use the chip brush to blend in the colors and blur the distinctions among them. If there are any bare spots, use the brush to drag the paint and cover them.

5- Next, move a whisk or flogger in an upward direction as you strike the surface to mark it with the hairs of the tool.
During this operation the whisk is used flat against the surface.

Sample on white background using natural umber, ultramarine blue, and white.

Sample on white background using light green, English green, and white.

6- Appearance of the finished project.

Oil stains for wood

Just as with water-based stains, oil stains are a simple and very effective finish that can be applied to create a variety of effects; they allow for mixing many colors, and since they take longer to dry, they give you more time to work.

You can use a single color or any number of colors that your imagination may call for; when they are mixed, they create an infinite variety of shades and gradations.

1- Mix one part linseed oil and two parts oil of turpentine, plus a couple drops of universal dryer. Dip a small sash brush into the mixture and saturate it with yellow coloring; apply this mixture unevenly by sections, leaving some areas uncovered.

2- In the same fashion, spread some orange onto different sections to cover up greater areas of untreated wood.

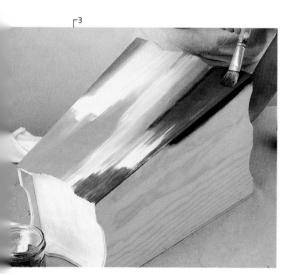

5- Finish unifying and blending the colors going over them with a paper towel in the direction of the grain to remove excess paint. Once the paint is dry, protect the project with two coats of oil-based satin-finish varnish. you're working on a piece of furniture that sees a lot of use, use polyurethane varnish.

3- Use ultramarine blue to cover up any areas that haven't yet been treated. If you want to create more shades, leave some areas uncovered; that way, when the colors are finalized, you'll get some lighter shades of different colors. When you use this technique to decorate a piece of furniture, work on one side at a time, completing one before moving on to the next; the colors are blended before they start to dry.

4- Use a chip brush to blend the colors together, moving the brush in the direction of the grain. There should not be any unsightly overlap lines where the colors meet.

6- Appearance of the finished project.

Sample using magenta, ultramarine blue, and emerald green.

Rag rolling

By using a rolled-up cotton rag to remove part of the paint that's been applied, you quickly and easily create an appearance of depth in the finish. You can use paints of one or more colors. This is a very fine procedure to use on large surfaces, even if they're uneven.

1- To prepare the glaze: mix one part linseed oil, two parts oil of turpentine, a few drops of universal dryer, and a half-tube of oil paint of the desired color, added gradually until you get the color you want.
Prepare the surface with a coat of neutral oil-based satin-finish paint. Spread the orange-colored glaze onto this surface in all directions. If you want to work with more than one color at the same time, alternate the colors by area.

3- Next, use the badger brush to blend in the brush marks left behind by the chip brush; move the brush in vertical figure eights over the surface.

4- Roll up a cotton rag to make a roller, making sure that you have kept some wrinkles in it. The tighter the rag is rolled, the more dramatic the effect.
Slide the roller in all directions as you press it down very gently onto the prepared surface. When the paint is dry, cover it with a coat of flat or satin-finish oil-based varnish.

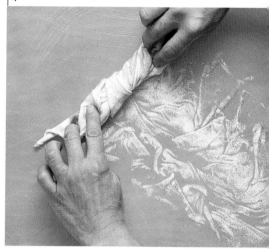

2- Using the chip brush, spread the glaze out evenly. Work the paint a little so it's well distributed over the entire surface.
If you're using more than one color, use a chip brush to soften the areas where they meet.

5- Finished appearance of the project.

Sample on a white and ultramarine blue background.

Sample on a light ochre and natural sienna background.

Tortoiseshell

For centuries people have used decorative painting to imitate the designs and shapes of tortoiseshell.

By applying a series of brush strokes on different colored backgrounds painted in advance, you can produce a very decorative finish that can be applied to small, flat surfaces to create a convincingly real effect, or to larger surfaces such as tables and lamp shades to create a very sophisticated finish with great visual impact.

1- Paint the entire surface you wish to decorate, previously treated with primer-sealer, with gold-colored acrylic paint and let it dry. If a single coat doesn't cover adequately, apply a second coat so that the surface is even all over. For this procedure use a natural-bristle brush. In olden times artisans used fine gold as a base when imitating tortoiseshell; nowadays, gold paints in various shades are used, plus yellows or reds depending on the type of finish that's desired.

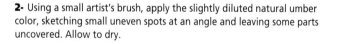

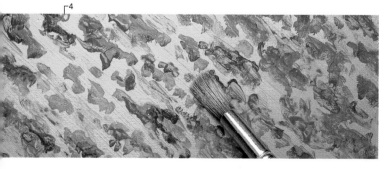

2- Using a small artist's brush, apply the slightly diluted natural umber color, sketching small uneven spots at an angle and leaving some parts uncovered. Allow to dry.

3- Repeat the same process with burnt sienna; apply paint over the first umber spots.
When you're done, let it dry.
To create a more convincing effect, the spots need to be irregular, and some parts should be left unpainted.

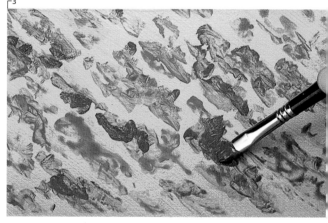

4- In order to be able to work with oils, varnish the whole surface using a small natural-bristle brush and glossy oil-based varnish; this will protect the acrylic colors. Let dry 24 hours.

5- Next, prepare a glaze by mixing one part linseed oil to two parts oil of turpentine; add some burnt umber oil coloring.
Spread this glaze over the entire surface using a natural-bristle brush.

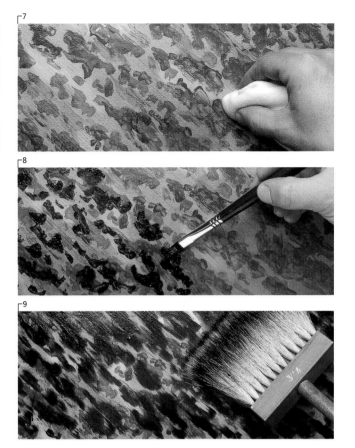

6- Use a chip brush to spread out the colored glaze and distribute it evenly over the entire surface.

7- Use a cotton cloth to rub through some areas and show the golden base color; this step creates an appearance of transparency and depth. These erasures need to be random and uneven, and to reveal some of the spots that were painted previously.

8- Before the glaze dries, make some more blotches on an angle and in a random pattern, using oil-base burnt umber mixed with black; this will produce different shades. The color is applied directly from the tube and mixed with the burnt umber glaze using a small artist's sash brush so that it melts into the surface.

9- Next, use a badger brush to blend the patterns, following the direction of the spots; the appearance should soften the borders between the colored spots and blend them together. Let dry.

10- Drying time for oil paints is difficult to predict; it depends on the surrounding temperature and humidity, and it can vary from two days to up to a couple of weeks.
Once the work is perfectly dry, apply a coat of glossy oil-based varnish. Tortoiseshell finish is very glossy, so it's appropriate to apply many coats of varnish to produce a very smooth finish. It's a good idea to apply at least five coats of glossy varnish, allowing adequate drying time between coats.

11- For a subdued, fine finish, moisten some fine-grit wet-or-dry sandpaper with water and lightly sand the surface between coats of varnish.

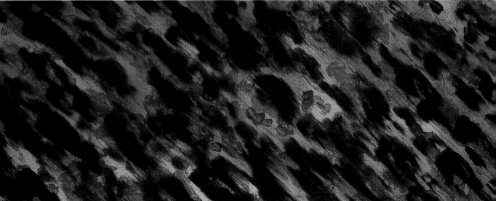

12- Appearance of the finished product.

Sky

Skies are always very attractive, and they have been used widely in decorative painting. The sense of depth that skies lend has led to their use on ceilings as well as on walls. In the past, many techniques were to used to represent skies. The following example produces spectacular results, but it's easy to do.

1- Prepare a light ultramarine blue glaze by mixing one part linseed c to two parts oil of turpentine. Spread the blue glaze onto a surfac previously prepared with satin-finish oil-based paint to cover areas abo 3 feet (1 m) square. The oil glaze takes a few hours to begin drying, b it's important to practice before starting to decorate large areas; if yc don't allow enough time to work the special effect, you may be able see the overlap lines between sections later on. In the ideal situatio you should be able to work on the entire surface that you're decoratin

2- Use a chip brush to spread the glaze over the entire area, keeping it as uniform as possible. This will avoid runs or drips when you're working on a wall.
If you want to cover a large area, it's a good idea to have two people working together; one can apply the paint and the other can even it ou

3- To blend in the brush marks that may remain from spreading the glaze with a chip brush, use a badger brush over the entire surface; that way the glaze will be perfectly integrated into the background. Use the badger brush in figure-eight patterns, holding it perpendicular to the surface and pressing very gently.

4- With a stippling (or equalizing) brush, tap the entire surface lightly to create a very subtle pitting effect that leaves the entire surface more uniform.
Use the equalizing brush whenever you want to create a surface that's even but with an appearance of depth. This effect is very well suited to creating a base for a sky. Sometimes, you may not want the entire base to be so even; in that case, you would equalize only certain areas.

5- Use a cotton cloth to erase some of the spread glaze in a cloud pattern; you create the clouds by rubbing through to the base coat. Before you begin, it's important to have a sketch of how you want the clouds to be distributed so you won't have to improvise. It's better to have a rough idea of how and where the designs will be distributed. If you suddenly forget what clouds look like, its a good idea to keep some magazine pictures or travel brochures on hand. Better yet, you can photograph different types of clouds in the sky. It's very helpful to have some examples to refer to.

6- In order to soften the effect produced by the cotton cloth, use the badger brush to blend it in. This will help you to integrate the appearance of the cloud with the sky. It's important to use real clouds as a point of reference and create some lighter areas and a sense of volume.

7- Use the equalizing (or stippling) brush to touch up the parts that are too light. When you're working on a vertical wall, you can create the appearance of greater depth if the blue is more intense higher up and lighter toward the area that would represent the horizon.

8- Appearance of the finished sky. For people with more experience or more courage, the color can be varied to produce red or golden skies, sunsets, or fantasy skies; you simply have to add some other colors to the background and integrate them using the equalizing (or stippling) brush and the badger brush.

Rustic wood

Painters and decorators use many types of finishes that imitate wood. A great number of imitations were being applied to lower-quality woods in doors and windows as early as the nineteenth century. Sometimes these were not copies of specific woods, but creating the appearance of grains and knots in bold colors produced some very attractive finishes.

The following exercise imitates a fairly dark wood, but it doesn't necessarily correspond to a particular type of wood. It's easy to do, and in rustic decors it lends a pleasant atmosphere; it's perfect for decorating beams, doors, and furniture.

1- Prepare a glaze by mixing one part linseed oil and two parts oil of turpentine; add a few drops of dryer, some natural dark umber pigment, and a little burnt umber to produce the desired color. Spread the glaze onto a surface previously prepared with oil-based satin-finish yellow ochre paint; use a sash brush and cover the entire area.

2- Use a chip brush to finish spreading out the glaze gently over the entire surface.
Wait a few minutes until the glaze becomes tacky.
To check if the glaze is at the right point to begin working, try to make some stripes on the surface and see if the brush marks blur. If they do, you have to wait a few minutes longer.

3- Fold up a piece of burlap so that you have flat surface; one of the edges will need to be straight.

4- Using the folded burlap and pressing the straight edge of the cloth onto the surface, slowly drag over the surface in one direction, rubbing off part of the glaze and making some irregular, fine lines; the base color will show through.

5- After you have striped the surface, go over it with a chip brush, following the direction of the lines; proceed gently and occasionally tap the surface with the brush to drag through the glaze; you want to make the lines a little more dynamic and keep them from being too straight. Let dry 24 hours.

6- Use the same glaze to apply another coat onto the entire project to deepen the color and create an appearance of depth.
You can use the same color glaze; but if you want something different, this is your chance to make an adjustment. This would be to darker colors, since lighter ones won't show against a dark background.

7- Use a chip brush to spread out the glaze so that the whole surface appears uniform, with an even coat all over.

Use a fine artist's brush and burnt umber loring to sketch some small spots of varying zes over the entire surface, as if they ere knots. Don't overdo this, or won't look attractive.

9- Use a cotton rag to make some gentle smears at the side of the knots and reveal some of the base color. This produces some subtle highlights that make the effect more convincing.

10- To create highlights, use the rag to erase some vertical bands; this keeps the finish from appearing too flat.

11- Use the chip brush to spread some glaze into the highlights of the knots, but without filling them in completely. This creates a subtle vertical shading on the underside; this shading around the highlights makes the knots look more real.

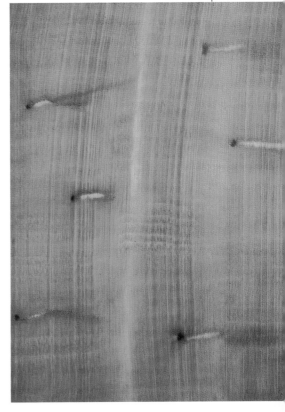

2- If you have any large blotches or ccumulations of glaze, use the chip brush to nooth them out and blend them into the ackground.

13- Use the chip brush to repeat the process of spreading some of the glaze by tamping it on the surface; this imitates curl in the wood grain and creates a little movement.

14- The appearance of the finished project. You can create different effects by using a different colored background.

Colorwashing

This technique is one more way to apply glazes or transparencies to create a subtle finish that's easy to do on large or small surfaces.

You can use a single color or mix various shades. The blending of the shades gives an appearance of depth to the decorated areas. If very high ceilings are decorated with dark colors, they appear lower; and if you use a dark colorwash near the floor and lighten it gradually, the colors create an impression of height.

This finish can be applied to uneven surfaces as long as they are prepared properly.

3- Next, dip the chip brush into a little glaze and into yellow ochre pigment; spread it out in all directions, leaving some spots uncovered. It's a good idea to make a little sketch of the area you're decorating so you get the color zones spread out properly and have an idea where to place each selected color.

1- Spread a transparent glaze in all directions over an entire surface previously painted with white oil-based satin-finish paint. The glaze consists of one part linseed oil and two parts oil of turpentine, plus a few drops of universal dryer.

2- Use the chip brush to spread the glaze ou over the entire surface and make sure there are no drips or uncovered spots.

3

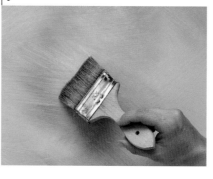

4- Using medium green paint, apply so spots to the open areas. If you are using m than two colors, alternate the different sha in different are

5- Use a sash brush to superimpose colors, spreading them out in all directions so that they are well integrated and cover the areas that are not painted.

6- Use gentle, short, overlapping strokes with the chip brush to blend in all directions. That way you integrate the colors of greater and lesser brightness so there are practically no borders between the blended shades.
If you want more intense colors, let dry well, up to two days, and apply a new coat of glaze to the areas where you want to emphasize the color. To produce a more durable finish, once it's dry, apply matte or satin-finish oil-based varnish.

Sample of burnt sienna and ultramarine blue on a white background.

7- Appearance of the finished proj

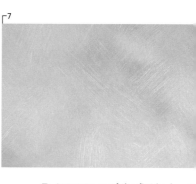

Sample of English red on a yellow ochre background.

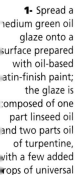

1- Spread a medium green oil glaze onto a surface prepared with oil-based satin-finish paint; the glaze is composed of one part linseed oil and two parts oil of turpentine, with a few added drops of universal dryer.

Imitation fabric

This is a technique that uses sweeping brush strokes; by applying a colored transparent glaze, you can create a soft impression of fine horizontal or vertical lines. Using this technique in conjunction with superimposed colors allows you to create the appearance of woven fabric; the result is very attractive.

2- Finish spreading out the glaze evenly with a chip brush used in a vertical direction.

3- Drag a bristle sash brush over the surface, also from top to bottom, to create a series of fine lines and let a little of the base coat show through. At the end of each drag, clean off the brush to get rid of any paint it has picked up and to keep the pattern clean. Let dry well.

4- Use a medium sash brush to spread ultramarine blue glaze over the entire area and cover it thoroughly.

5- Spread the glaze out evenly using a chip brush.

7- Appearance of the finished project.

- Next, drag the long-haired sash brush horizontally and at right angles to the previous direction; at the same time, press down with your hand. This produces more contrast, and the striping is more irregular; it looks like a different weave in each line.

This finish is very attractive on furniture that has flat surfaces, and on wainscoting on walls. By choosing bold colors you can create some very artistic fabric effects.

Veined white marble

In decorative painting, imitations of marble transport us to the era of the Romans, where a great variety of styles were used.

It's easy to imitate veined white marble by applying paint to different surfaces, from small pieces to baseboards and even floors. With proper results, marble gives rooms a certain classical elegance and sobriety.

1- Prepare a colorless glaze by mixing one part linseed oil and two parts oil of turpentine. Then spread the glaze onto a surface previously painted with white satin-finish oil-based paint.

2- Use a chip brush to spread out the colorless glaze evenly.

3- Mix up a light gray paint with some white and a little black; next, mix it with a little colorless glaze and make some subtle blotches at an angle on the surface, creating some cloudy shapes. This marble is distinctive because its spots and veins are always arranged on a diagonal.

4- Use a badger-hair brush to blend in the spots gently and integrate them with the background in a cloudy fashion. Move the brush in figure eights so you can integrate the spot without displacing it.

5- Prepare a shade of gray slightly darker than the first one by using a little ultramarine blue; go over the spots again and darken some of them.

7- Dip the fine artist's veining brush into dark gray coloring and sketch out some subtle, somewhat broken veins on a slant so that they look natural.

6- Then gently blend with the badger-hair brush to melt the blotches together and create depth. You have to blend very subtly; you don't want to erase entirely the cloudy appearance of the blotches.

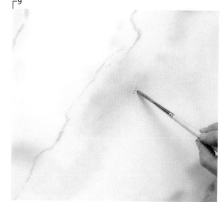

8- Smooth out the veins with the badger-hair brush; move it in only one direction to integrate the veins with the background colors. It's more attractive if the lines that denote the veins are somewhat broken and vary in width and intensity from beginning to end.

9- Using the same dark gray color, draw some small clusters of dots to simulate the fossils that this marble contains. Paint groups of seven or a dozen dots, some of them in the shape of a half-moon.

10- Use the badger-hair brush to blend in the clusters of dots and integrate them with the background. As you do this, move the brush in figure eights so you don't distort the image.

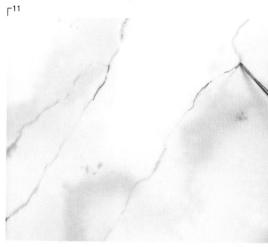

11- Dip the veining brush in a little dark gray and reinforce some sections of the veins to give them more depth and different tonal values.

12- Finally, use the badger-hair brush to blend in the sections that stand out too strongly, and create a more harmonious whole.

13- Appearance of the finished project. You can create different effects by varying the background color; instead of white, you can work on a pink background, or on a soft blue. You can also produce different finishes by using colors other than grays.

Malachite

There are a great many semiprecious stones that are used in decorating, and one of them is malachite. In most cases it would be very costly to use the real material, so for centuries people have used paint to imitate it.

To achieve more convincing results, you should work in small areas. If you need to cover large areas, it's better to divide them into small sections to produce a much more real appearance.

You can decorate anything from large columns to small table objects, especially with the help of imitation marquetry.

1- Prepare a transparent glaze by mixing one part linseed oil to two parts oil of turpentine and a few drops of universal dryer.
Spread the transparent glaze in all directions on a surface painted with light bluish green oil-based satin-finish paint; use a small brush for this operation.

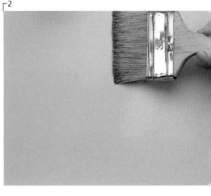

2- Next, use a chip brush to spread it out well and ensure that the transparent glaze covers the entire surface.

3- With oil colors, you next smear most of the surface with green from the paint tube, leaving small areas uncovered. In these places you apply spots of ultramarine blue and raw umber. Make unequal splotches and leave some small spots uncovered.

4- Cut out some pieces of corrugated cardboard in different widths and drag them over the painted surface to create some circular patterns and mix the colors together. As you drag the cardboard, wiggle it just a bit to put a little twist into the pattern. Next, let dry.

5- Mix a glaze using some green from the paint tube and a little black; spread this over the entire area that you painted previously and that is now dry

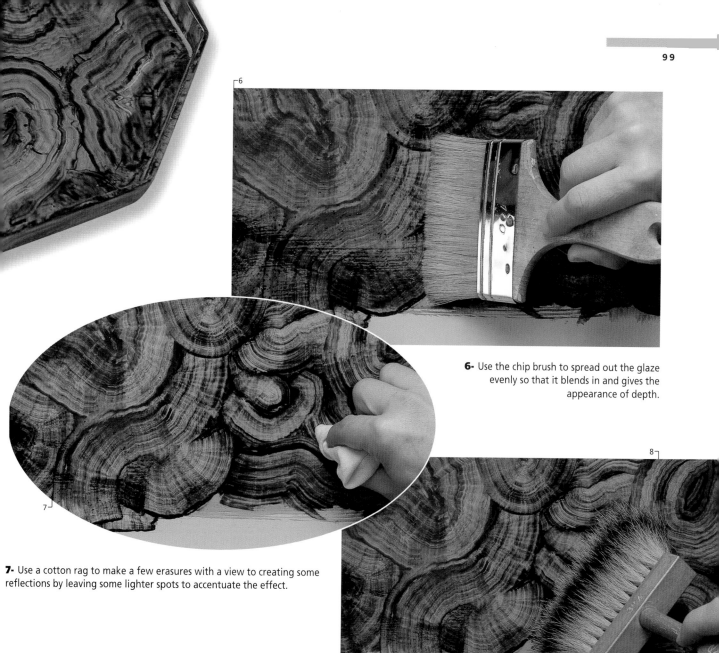

6- Use the chip brush to spread out the glaze evenly so that it blends in and gives the appearance of depth.

7- Use a cotton rag to make a few erasures with a view to creating some reflections by leaving some lighter spots to accentuate the effect.

8- Use the badger-hair brush to smooth over the area, blend the light effects with the background and disguise the brush marks.

9- Appearance of the finished project. It's always easier to create more convincing imitations if you locate and study a piece of malachite to see the twisting forms that characterize this mineral.

Fantasy marble

Imitations of marble have been used in decorating in nearly all ages. There are many types of marble that can be used as models.

In this marble finish, you can give your imagination free rein in creating decorative effects; it has been used to combine a variety of effects and colors.

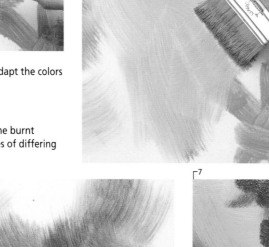

1- Prepare a transparent glaze consisting of one part linseed oil, two parts oil of turpentine, and a few drops of universal dryer. Spread the glaze onto a surface painted with white satin-finish oil-based paint; use a sash brush to paint it on in all directions.

2- Use a chip brush to spread the glaze out and cover the entire area, leaving no uncovered spots.

3- Prepare a palette with oil colors. Dip an artist's brush in a little glaze then in a little yellow ochre pigment and apply some uneven blotches to different areas.

4- Use the chip brush to spread out the paint, expanding the blotches and blending them into the background. Leave some areas colored more darkly.

5- Next, using a medium artist's brush, apply some spots of English red to other areas and try to integrate the two colors.

6- Use the chip brush again to adapt the colors to the background.

7- With an artist's brush and some burnt umber, make some small blotches of differing intensity in certain areas.

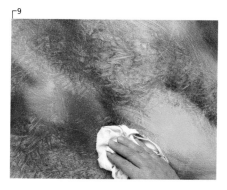

8- Integrate the new color with the previous ones by spreading it out and blending it in with a chip brush.

9- Use a cotton rag to press and rub the surface gently and leave some small marks in certain places; leave other areas untouched.

10- Use the badger-hair brush to blend the paint by moving it in figure eights as you hold it perpendicular to the surface.

11- Cut a plastic bag into pieces and crumple them up so that they have lines going across them; next, press the plastic onto certain areas to produce a contrast with the background. The markings you produce with the plastic can be quite varied, depending on the thickness of the plastic. The plastic must not be too stiff.

12- Gently use the badger-hair brush to blend in the most obvious markings and the entire effect in general. The brush is used to integrate the various effects, but you have to be careful not to erase them entirely.

13- Moisten a synthetic sponge in transparent glaze and press it onto certain areas so that it leaves an impression of its texture; this produces a marbling effect.
You can use sponges of different textures, with different-size holes, and natural sponges. The latter leave different types of marks, but they too are very effective.

14- Use the badger-hair brush to smooth out the marks. You can also use the badger-hair brush to erase some pattern that doesn't look quite right.

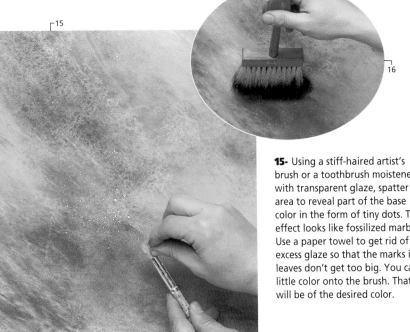

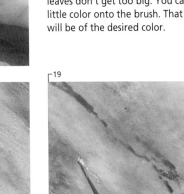

15- Using a stiff-haired artist's brush or a toothbrush moistened with transparent glaze, spatter an area to reveal part of the base color in the form of tiny dots. This effect looks like fossilized marble. Use a paper towel to get rid of excess glaze so that the marks it leaves don't get too big. You can also mix a little color onto the brush. That way the spots will be of the desired color.

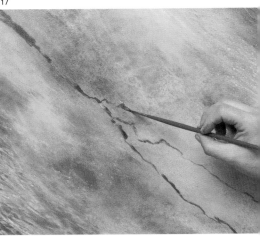

16- Use the badger-hair brush to smooth out the spots and keep them from spreading and becoming too large.

17- With a fine artist's brush paint on some very thin veins in burnt umber. Use the background as a point of reference and sketch the veins on a diagonal.

18- Next, integrate the veins with the background, using the badger-hair brush to blend them in, following the direction of the sketched veins.

19- Also sketch in some small, fine secondary veins to emulate small channels of calcified water and make the marble effect more convincing.

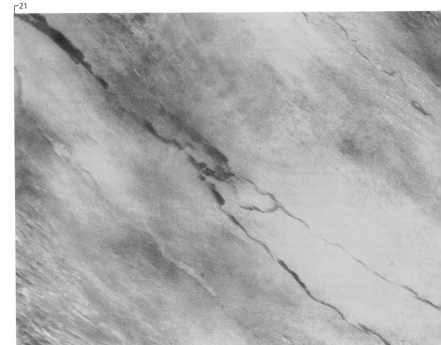

20- Once again use the badger-hair brush to blend in the small veins and integrate them into the whole scheme.

21- Appearance of the finished project.

Faux Venetian stucco

One of the most widely used techniques in decorating large areas is oil ragging. This effect is a visual reminder of ancient Venetian stuccos, but in practice it is much easier to create and more economical.

1- Prepare a glaze using one part linseed oil, two parts oil of turpentine, a few drops of universal dryer, and a half-tube of oil paint of the desired color; add color until you get the shade you want.

Using a medium sash brush, spread the glaze out in all directions on a surface previously painted with two coats of pink satin-finish enamel.

The glaze needs to be transparent, so don't load the brush up with too much color; otherwise you'll lose the effect of transparency.

2- Using a chip brush, finish spreading out the color evenly over the entire surface.
It's a good idea to work in irregularly shaped areas about 3 feet (1 m) on a side. The advantage you have in working with oils is that the drying time is longer, and that allows you to eliminate the appearance of joints where the glaze overlaps.

3- Using a piece of cotton cloth, make a dabber that's about the size of your hand. Start by marking the impression of the rag in all directions, trying to avoid repeating patterns. Depending on the wrinkles in the cloth, the marks will take on a certain shape.

4- Use the badger-hair brush to smooth out the treated area, blending very gently by moving the brush in a figure-eight movement. The blending done with the badger-hair brush needs to be very subtle; if you press too hard you may erase the effect you created in the previous step. Once it's dry, you can darken the color by repeating the same operation.
You can also use a different color. To protect the project, let it dry and apply two coats of varnish—matte or satin depending on the type of finish you want.

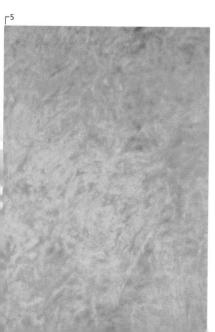

5- Appearance of the finished project.

Sample of raw sienna glaze on a light ochre background.

Travertine marble

Many marbles present an infinite variety of shades and veins, but others look almost like stone with small holes and different shades within the same spectrum of color. The type of marble that presents a lighter appearance is commonly used for large areas and for floors.

This oil technique allows you to create truly decorative finishes very simply.

1- Prepare a glaze by mixing one part linseed oil, two parts oil of turpentine, plus raw umber and a little white. Spread this onto a surface previously painted with off-white satin-finish oil-based paint.

2- In certain spaces on the surface, mark off some stripes of unequal width in burnt sienna.

3- Blend the colors into one another, passing a chip brush lightly over the surface; keep the brush moving in one direction so that the colors integrate without erasing.

4- Crumple up a small piece of paper and use a brush to fill the largest wrinkles with burnt umber.

5- Use the wrinkled paper to press lightly onto the surface, leaving small, uneven marks of differing intensity. You'll have to keep changing the paper and refilling the wrinkles so that the effect is different each time.

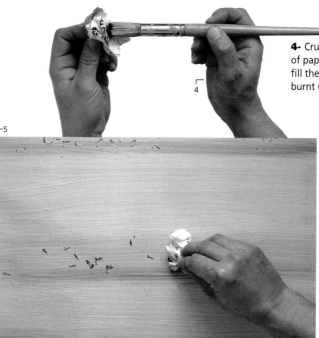

6- To integrate various dark shades, subtly smooth and blend everything by using the badger-hair brush in figure-eight motions.

7- Cut some sections of fine plastic wrap and wrinkle it on the sides, making small horizontal folds. Apply these onto the surface horizontally, pressing with some force by passing your hands over the plastic.

8- Very carefully pull back the plastic sheet, and repeat the process over the entire surface you're decorating.

The visual impression of this imitation marble is more convincing if you work in blocks no larger than about 36 inches long by 24 inches wide (90 x 60 cm). That will produce a more natural result.

9- If the marks from the plastic are too noticeable, go over them with the badger-hair brush to blend them in with the background. Let dry at least 24 hours.

10- To create greater depth in this effect, once the paint is thoroughly dry, spread a very transparent raw umber glaze over the entire surface.

You have to be absolutely sure that the paint is dry before applying the next glaze. Sometimes projects painted with oils take a long time to dry, depending on the climate and the surrounding temperature.

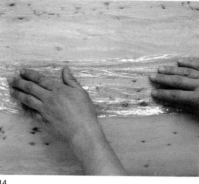

11- Spread out the glaze with a chip brush; make sure that the entire surface is covered uniformly.

12- Once again you can apply the plastic to certain areas as indicated earlier to allow some of the base color to show through.

You can also use thicker plastic to produce more exaggerated effects.

13- Use the badger-hair brush to blend in the surface using figure-eight motions to integrate the effects with the background.

Whenever you use the badger-hair brush for blending, you must be gentle to avoid erasing the effect; if you use the brush too much, you can make the desired effect disappear entirely. Let dry at least 24 hours; then protect the finish with two coats of satin-finish oil-based varnish.

14- Appearance of the finished project.

Mahogany palm

It looks difficult to master the techniques for imitating certain woods. Since the seventeenth century, painters have been using their skills to create imitations that are so convincing it's hard to tell the difference merely by looking—especially in the case of exotic woods. It's a good idea to study the woods you want to imitate, or to have some samples or photos on hand while you paint.

There are several different types of mahogany. Red mahogany is the most exotic, with a background of reddish orange; golden mahogany sometimes was imitated by painting on top of gold leaf. The part that makes up the palm of mahogany is the most attractive and decorative, and this is what we will try to reproduce in the following exercise.

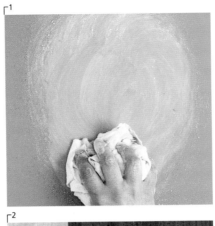

1- This effect is created in two steps, one using a water technique, and the second with oil. Pass a cotton rag moistened with Spanish white over a surface previously prepared with bright orange alkyd paint; rub vigorously so that the water-based paint will stick to this base.
Alkyd paint is an oil-based paint, and a water-based paint normally doesn't adhere to it very well. Spanish white acts as a degreaser and makes the surface more receptive to water-based paint.

2- Mix some red paint with a little black to produce a dark brown color. To keep the paint from becoming too thick, add water in the proportion of one part paint to two parts water.
This produces a slightly transparent paint. Next, use a medium sash brush to spread the paint onto the surface in a vertical direction. This step has to be done quickly so that the paint doesn't dry.

3- Use the chip brush to spread the paint out evenly. Here too you have to work quickly so that the paint doesn't dry.
If the paint should dry before you have a chance to work it, you can add a little more water to extend the drying time. If the paint dries part-way through the process, you can quickly rub the surface with alcohol to get rid of the dry paint. In this case you would have to apply the Spanish white again.

4- Cut off one side of a synthetic sponge with a hobbyist's knife to get an edge that's as straight as possible.
Dampen the sponge slightly and start dragging the glazes from low to high toward the middle of the palm, leaving a small accumulation of color in the middle. From this point on, continue in the same fashion from high to low, creating the shape of what will turn into the palm of mahogany. Let dry 20 minutes.

5- Using a sash brush for varnish, spread a thin, even coat of satin-finish oil-based varnish. Next, let dry for 24 hours.

6- Mix up a dark reddish brown paint using carmine red, black, and a little ultramarine blue oil color; mix this with a transparent glaze made by mixing one part linseed oil and two parts oil of turpentine, plus a few drops of universal dryer.

7- Using a chip brush, gently spread out the paint to produce an even coat.

8- To eliminate the brush marks left by the chip brush, use the badger-hair brush in figure-eight motions to blend the surface. This will allow the previous design to show through.

9- Moisten a long-haired bristle brush with transparent glaze and shake off the excess glaze before beginning. Apply the glaze by following certain sections of the first pattern to create some highlights.
It's important that the sash brush not have much glaze on it; otherwise the light effect would be too obvious.

10- Use the badger-hair brush to smooth out the effect and integrate it naturally into the whole.

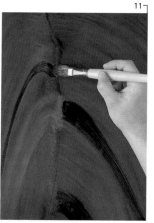

11- Prepare a darker color using red and black paints; use an artist's bristle sash brush to draw some darker areas to accentuate the changes among different shades; follow the curves that are still transparent. Then blend in the whole surface with the badger-hair brush.

12- With a smaller artist's sash brush, create some subtle light effects next to some of the dark areas to heighten the contrast.

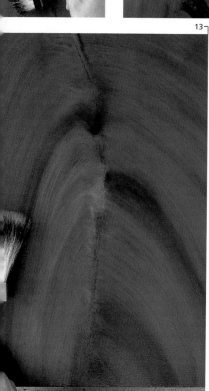

13- Gently use the badger-hair brush to blend the whole scheme together in the areas outside the palm from low to high. Tap lightly with the brush as you move upward to create some subtle marks similar to the pores of wood. Let dry 24 hours and top with two coats of satin-finish varnish; let dry between coats. This step is similar to whisking except that it's used only outside the palm and in a very subtle and subdued manner.

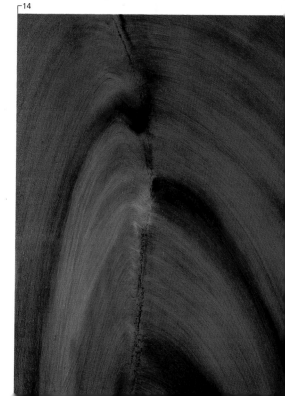

14- Appearance of the finished project.

Wax scumbling

This technique uses scumbling, but with the difference that in this exercise we use wax in metallic colors to produce a very decorative finish, especially on small pieces and furniture.

1- Prepare the surface you want to decorate by applying one coat of acrylic primer-sealer; use a medium sash brush and let the object dry.

2- Once the object is dry, paint it with dark brown paint, making sure to cover it thoroughly. If necessary, once the first coat is dry, brush on a second coat. Let dry again.

3- Paint the whole surface unevenly with English red paint; leave some areas in the previous color. You can use different colors for the base coat, one on top of another and applied unevenly; after scumbling, they'll be visible again.

4- Using a nearly dry sash brush, apply some medium green paint by using small, elongated brush strokes on different parts of the piece.

5- Once the piece is dry, apply some pewter-colored wax with a stiff brush, gradually covering the entire surface. Wait 24 hours for the wax to dry thoroughly.

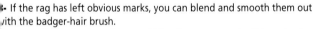

6- Use medium-grit steel wool to rub the entire surface, emphasizing the high spots. This allows the base colors to show through. This must be done unevenly to give the finish a more natural look. Depending on the effect you want to produce, you can either scrub the object or scratch it.

7- In a shallow container, dilute the dark brown acrylic paint by adding an equal amount of water. Use this mixture to cover the piece a section at a time and quickly remove the excess with a cotton cloth.
You can use any color you want to cover the scumble, but you can apply any other dark color such as black, ultramarine blue, and others, to age the piece.

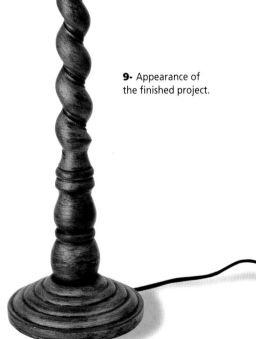

8- If the rag has left obvious marks, you can blend and smooth them out with the badger-hair brush.
If you get the desired result by scrubbing the wax, you don't have to do this step to darken it.

9- Appearance of the finished project.

6 Patinas

A patina is the color and texture that the surface of a material acquires naturally through the effects of erosion and the passage of time. These visual effects can be reproduced by using paints and different materials.

Some of the patinas that are presented in the following pages represent the various types of oxidation of some metals; others suggest the distressed, almost damaged appearance that some pieces take on as the years go by. Some finishes for oxidizing or aging, and others that are more fantastic, are almost magic when they're applied to practically any surface.

Decorating with patinas

Often the beauty of decorated objects is the result of applying various decorative patinas. Nowadays pieces and objects are used increasingly to complement decors; previously they were used more as decorations for movie sets and in display windows.

By mastering these techniques and experimenting with different materials, you can transform simple objects, including ones with no inherent esthetic value, into impressive decorative pieces.

Applications

There are many possible applications, and although they can be used on different types of surfaces, large, smooth walls can be fairly difficult unless you have a certain amount of experience.

On furniture, small objects, and architectural pieces, the effects can be quite astonishing. They are applied basically to transform and give the appearance of different materials, creating an optical illusion and reproducing different metal finishes or materials that have been transformed by the passage of time.

Practically all types of paint can be used: vinyl, acrylic, oil . . . and for base materials: talc, ash, and marble dust. Any material, no matter how strange it may seem, can serve to create some spectacular finishes. Many painters, and metal sculptors especially, use various acids to create effects, but since many of them can be very toxic, we have limited our selection to materials and products that are harmless.

Plaster pieces decorated with different aged finishes. Verdigris (A), old silver (B), blue and gold (C), aged oxidized gilding (D), graphite (E), polychrome (F), bronze (G), ivory (H), distressed terra-cotta (I), oxide of iron sulfate (J), and oxidized gold (K).

Decorative effects

The various patinas are used to intentionally create the characteristic tones that the passage of time gives to paintings, sculptures, and other types of objects; used as decorative effects, patinas provide depth when they obscure twists and turns and highlight raised areas. Today there are many commercial products that are designated as patinas. These products, which are more or less transparent and are used in superimposing shades and colors, can be useful, but many times they are much too costly. Here, using more common materials (some of which can be found in most households), we will offer different tricks for creating effects that decorative painters use.

Many times the type of patina that's chosen is determined by the type of piece, its shape, and its texture, which sometimes is a clue as to how it should be treated to make it more attractive.

Corbel decorated with imitation gold leaf and aged.

Where to apply patinas

As with all the previous techniques, this one can be applied in many different ways; the important thing is to work on surfaces that are prepared correctly for every instance or visual effect. Sometimes, certain patinas can be produced directly on pieces of plaster, but only in the case of a very concrete finish such as wax or asphaltum being used to simulate aged stone. On the other hand, other patinas will require adequate preparation for each type of finish desired. The base materials can be quite varied: iron, plaster, wood, resins, and Styrofoam, for example, and each one is prepared with a specific primer-sealer.

You have to keep in mind that if the pieces, objects, furniture, and so forth that you want to decorate have relief or carving, it will be a lot easier to create the effects for which patinas are best suited.

Frames for mirrors or pictures, architectural pieces, large or small sculptures, and furniture are ideal candidates for treatment with these techniques. Observation and study of old pieces to see where they are most distressed or where oxidation is most visible will help you create more convincing effects of aging. For example, with a piece of furniture that has drawers, the drawers are treated with a lighter patina than the corners or the bas-relief, where the surface is darker because it's not subject to wear.

So to master the technique of aging pieces through the use of patinas, it's important to examine real pieces and objects so the effects you create are more natural looking.

Classical pieces are ideal for transforming with patinas; this plaster bust has been aged using a patina of asphaltum and wax with talc.

Metal reflections

The multiple combinations that can be created by applying patinas yield great beauty when they are given a touch of metallic reflection by means of metallic wax.

Iron effect

The effect of cast iron gives any surface, whether of plaster, plastic, or any other material, the appearance of this material by means of a simple but spectacular application of color.

1- Apply an even coat of medium gray acrylic paint to a plaster piece prepared with acrylic primer-sealer. Let dry 15 minutes.

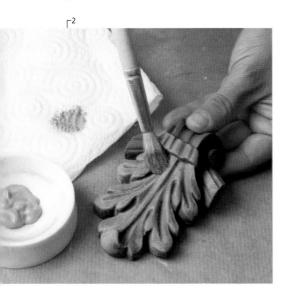

2- Proceed to paint certain areas lightly without covering the first color completely. Let dry ten minutes.

3- With a flat stenciling brush, take up a little dark gray acrylic paint and blot the excess on a piece of paper towel. Shade in the whole piece, paying particular attention to some areas in relief, taking care not to cover entirely the colors applied previously. Let dry ten minutes.

4- Take a little pewter-colored metallic wax on the pads of your fingers and apply it unevenly to some of the raised portions of the piece. Let dry a half-hour.

5- Use a soft cloth or a smooth chamois to polish the wax and create the metallic reflections that make the piece look like iron.

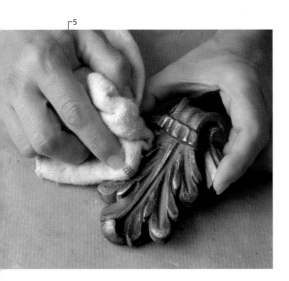

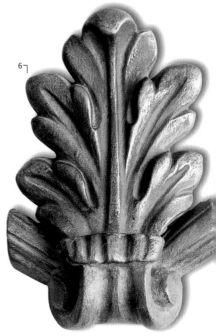

6- Appearance of the finished piece.

Blue and gold effect

These effects turn out best on pieces that have bas-relief, and they are very decorative on all pieces, large or small. Other combinations of colors can also be very attractive.

1- Prepare the piece with acrylic primer-sealer and let it dry. Paint the whole piece with Prussian blue; apply a second coat if necessary to cover the piece thoroughly. Let dry a half-hour.

2- Next, use a small brush to apply light blue oil color, emphasizing the raised areas.

3- Use a piece of cotton rag to wipe off excess paint, paying particular attention to the raised areas so that the background color shows through and the piece has more shades of color. Let dry two hours.

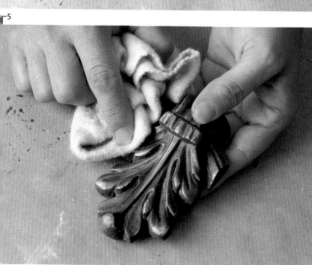

4- Using gold-colored gilding wax applied with the pad of a finger, highlight certain raised areas. The amount of golden highlights depends on your personal taste and the result you want to create. Let dry a half-hour.

5- Once the piece is dry, polish it by rubbing it gently with a soft cloth or smooth chamois.

6- Appearance of the finished piece.

Old wood effect

Although we are attempting to create metallic effects, this exercise makes it easy to transform any object of plastic, plaster, resin, and so forth into a nobler material such as wood. This patina is used to produce the appearance of old wood.

1- Paint the entire surface of the object to be decorated—previously prepared with acrylic primer-sealer—with beige paint. Let dry ten minutes.

2- Load the brush with black acrylic paint, blotting the excess on a paper towel; lightly shade in the relief, letting some of the base color show through. Let dry ten minutes.

3- Next, apply a fairly thick dark brown glaze to the entire piece. Let dry 20 minutes.

4- Before the glaze is totally dry, cover the entire piece with talcum powder, paying particular attention to the corners and cut-outs; let dry ten minutes.

5- Use a dry brush to get rid of the excess talc, leaving just a little in the corners.

6- Next, use a soft cloth to remove a little more of the talc that still clings to the high spots; this lets some of the background colors show through.

7- To highlight some parts of the relief areas and the shapes you want to accentuate, use the pad of your finger to apply some light touches of light golden metallic wax. Let dry for a half-hour.

8- Rub lightly with a chamois cloth to make the metallic shine more visible.

9- The appearance of the finished piece.

Garnet and copper effect

The right combination of colors is the most important thing when working with aging patinas. You can even create some very rich effects by changing the shades of the gilding waxes and using them in greater quantities to cover more area.

1- Prepare the piece with acrylic primer-sealer and let dry two hours. Paint the whole piece with an even coat of medium garnet paint. Let dry a half-hour.

2- Cover the surface of the piece with light green oil glaze, paying particular attention to the corners and bas-reliefs.

3- Wipe off the excess glaze from the high spots with a chamois cloth; this will give the piece some different shades of color. Let dry a half-hour.

4- Use a stenciling brush to take up a little medium garnet paint, removing any excess with paper towel; next, shade in the piece and accentuate some of the raised areas. Let dry ten minutes.

5- Take a little copper-colored wax on the pad of your finger and give a shine to the whole piece, rubbing the high spots more. Let dry a half-hour.

6- Use a chamois cloth to polish the whole piece gently to the point where you're satisfied with the shine.

7- Appearance of the finished piece.

Oxidized gold effect

Asphaltum mixed with wax is an aging patina that can be used to create practically any effect; you can also use shoe polish in lighter shades to produce decorative finishes. You merely need to experiment with it.

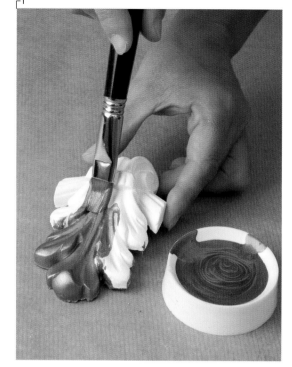

1- Apply primer-sealer to the entire piece and let dry two hours. Paint the whole object with acrylic yellow gold paint. Put on a second coat so that the piece is covered uniformly. Some acrylic metallic colors don't cover very well; that's why several coats are often used.

2- Next, cover the piece a section at a time with light green acrylic paint; pay particular attention to the bas-relief.

3- Quickly wipe off excess paint using a cotton cloth, leaving some areas lighter than others.

4- Use a mixture of clear wax and asphaltum as you apply a patina unevenly over the entire piece.

5- Dab the piece with a soft cloth to get rid of excess patina and create some lighter areas. If you need to remove excess patina in the bas-relief, use a dry brush. Let dry one hour.

6- Highlight the piece by applying an uneven coat of yellow gold metallic wax to the raised areas with your finger. Let dry a half-hour.
Use a chamois cloth or a soft cloth to polish the whole piece, especially the high spots, to make it more attractive.

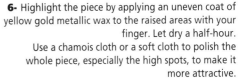

7- Appearance of the finished piece.

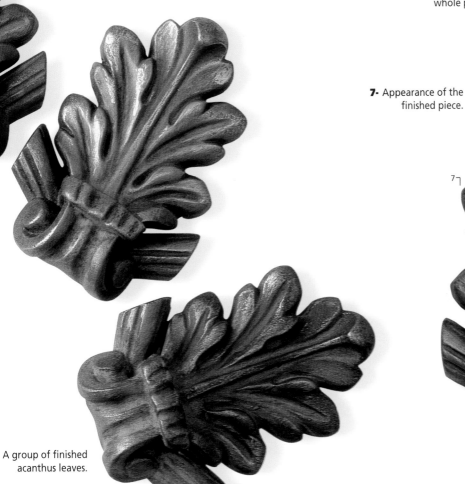

A group of finished acanthus leaves.

Old stone patina

Often it's very easy to transform objects by using an aging patina to create a great final effect. The best material for this type of finish is plaster, since its porous nature contributes to the convincing final appearance. There are many architectural pieces and sculptures made of this material that take on great beauty when they're treated with this finish.

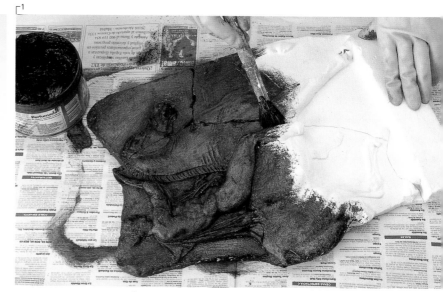

1- Clean all the dust off the piece of plaster you have chosen to decorate. Prepare a mixture of one part furniture wax and one part asphaltum and use a brush to cover the entire piece with it, being especially careful in the bas-relief areas. If you want to decorate another type of material with this finish, such as plastic, wood, Styrofoam, or others, first put on a coat of primer suited to the material, followed by two coats of matte acrylic paint; this will produce a porous base similar to plaster. To be sure that the finish is right, first do a test on some part that won't be visible.

2- Before the patina dries, use a soft cotton cloth to remove the excess from certain areas, particularly the high spots. To remove excess patina in the bas-relief areas, use a dry brush to reach into the corners that are inaccessible with the cloth.

3- If the piece is too uniform or too dark, lighten the patina by rubbing it with a rag impregnated with clear wax; this will lighten the dark areas. The patina won't be the same shade throughout the entire piece. Sometimes you want areas that are much darker than others; if that's the case, don't lighten them.

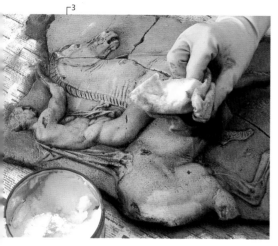

4- Before the wax begins to dry, cover the whole piece with talcum powder. The talc softens the contrast provided by the patina and leaves the piece with a very soft and delicate feel.

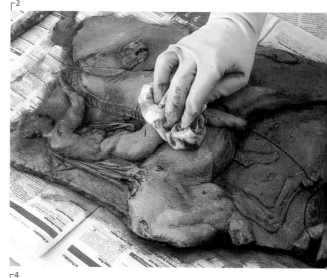

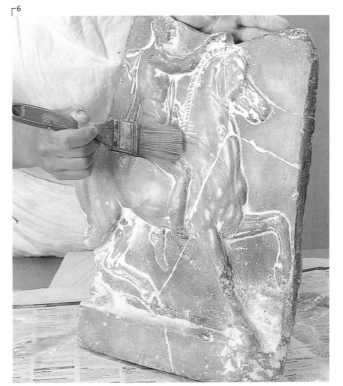

- Next, spread the talc out on the piece with your hands, rubbing gently so that it gets into every nook and cranny. Let dry 24 hours so that the talc will stick in the wax. You can get industrial talc in some specialty shops, but you can also use the scented talc—it's simply more expensive.

6- Use a dry bristle brush to remove the excess talc from the piece; leave just a little in the bas-relief to make the appearance of ancient stone more convincing.

- Buff the piece with a chamois cloth or a soft rag, rubbing gently until the piece takes on a very attractive, pleasing, silky touch and appearance.

8- Appearance of the finished piece.

Graphite

Graphite is a mineral, crystallized carbon, of dark gray color. It's rarely used as a coloring pigment, but it's commonly used when a high-quality texture is desired. Graphite can also be used to create very decorative finishes that look like metal. It's also the primary material used in the manufacture of pencil leads.

1- Apply a thorough coat of acrylic primer-sealer on the entire piece and let dry two hours. Once it's dry, cover the piece with an even coat of oil-based satin-finish paint. Let dry until tacky. You can tell if it has dried to the right point by lightly touching the surface; it should feel sticky, but it shouldn't come off on your fingers. This is the stage at which the paint is said to be tacky.

2- Take up a little graphite on a small, dry bristle brush and sprinkle it over the entire piece until it's completely covered, making sure it gets into the bas-relief. Let dry 24 hours. If the piece you're decorating is fairly sizable and has no flat surfaces, you can spread out the graphite by tapping lightly with a sash brush to make the powder stick to the surface.

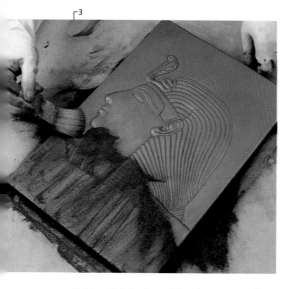

3- Use a totally dry sash brush to remove the excess graphite, brushing gently to remove everything that's loose.

4- Use a chamois cloth or a soft cloth to buff the piece and beautify the effect. The slightly grainy texture of pieces that are finished with graphite is very attractive.

5- Appearance of the finished piece.

Gum lacquer and calcic wax

Calcic wax is a mixture of beeswax and white pigment. The off-white tint you get when you use it as a glaze is different from what you usually experience, since it's used to darken pieces and make them look older. The finish you get when you use this wax makes the piece look old but very beautiful.

1- Apply a coat of clear gum lacquer as a primer-sealer to the entire surface of the imitation marble piece that has been cleaned thoroughly. Let dry and apply a second coat. Drying time is 15 minutes.
It's important that the piece be very clean and spotless, since the transparent coating won't cover any imperfections or scratches.

2- Gum lacquer comes in different shades, from clear to dark but transparent shades; it can also be tinted with pigments. In this case, the gum lacquer is tinted with burnt sienna pigment to produce an orange shade. Apply several coats of orange gum lacquer, allowing 15 minutes' drying time between coats. If you want a brighter color, put on more coats of gum lacquer so that the shade darkens with every coat; however, don't sacrifice the transparent quality of the finish. Let dry one hour.

3- Use a bristle brush to apply a coat of calcic wax to the entire surface of the piece; make sure you get some wax into the bas-relief.

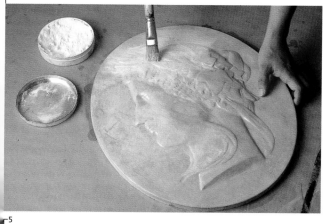

4- Once you have finished applying the calcic wax, use a brush held vertically to tap the surface lightly and eliminate any brush marks that may be left over from applying the wax. The surface should look as if it's lightly stippled all over. Let dry 30 minutes.

5- Using fine steel wool, rub the areas where you want the base color to show through. Rub very carefully by sections to produce an uneven shade throughout the piece. If the wax has dried too much and is difficult to remove, rub the area gently with a rag containing a little clear wax; this will help get rid of the excess.
You can finish up by buffing with a soft rag until the piece feels smooth and silky.

6- Appearance of the finished piece.

Polychrome

Applying color to decorative pieces and ornamental architectural elements is a technique that has been used in almost all ages and styles. If aging patinas are also applied, the objects will have a smoother and more harmonious finish.

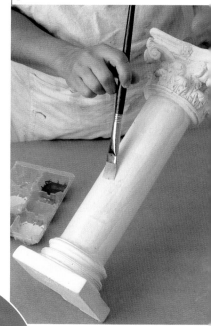

1- Apply a coat of gum lacquer diluted to a 50% solution with alcohol to a plaster piece from which all dust has been removed; in this case the gum lacquer seals the porous surface of the plaster and makes it slippery. If the piece absorbs the gum lacquer quickly and leaves some porous areas, apply a second coat.

2- Acrylic colors are mixed with water in the proportion of one part paint to two of water; this makes them like watercolors. Start decorating by applying a neutral color to the whole column.

3- Paint a portion of the ornamentation in the capital with light green paint, leaving some areas practically transparent. If you prefer colors that are more opaque, apply more coats of the paint, allowing adequate drying time between coats.

4- The base of the small column is painted garnet color. It's a good idea to use darker colors for the base in the interest of balance in the entire piece.

5- The top of the capital is painted with very diluted Prussian blue.

6- To harmonize with the color of the base, a portion of the capital is painted garnet.

7- Paint the edgings of the column and the base of the capital with undiluted yellow gold paint; these small details set off the final finish. Let the whole piece dry thoroughly for two hours.

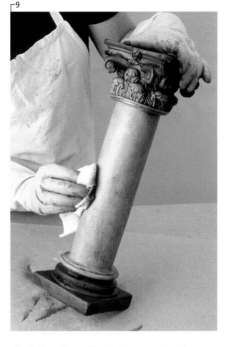

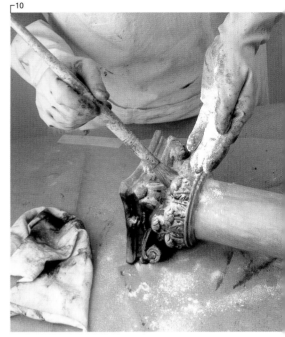

- Apply a coat of asphaltum with wax over the entire piece, dabbing lightly with the brush to eliminate any brush strokes that may remain.

- Gently dab with a soft cotton cloth to remove excess asphaltum and spread it out more uniformly over the entire piece.

10- Before the patina dries, cover the piece with talc and use a small brush to fill up the bas-relief.
On the curved sections, where it's harder to get the talc to stick, press it on with your hands. Let dry two hours.

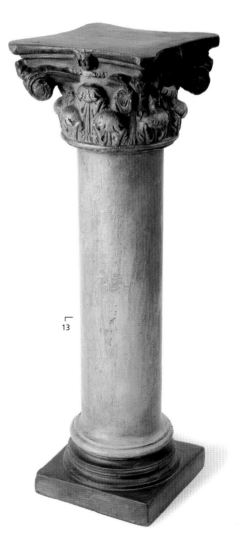

- Remove the leftover talc with a dry brush, paying particular attention to the bas-0relief.

12- Rub the whole piece gently with a chamois cloth to make the background colors stand out more and look more lively. This will produce a smooth, satiny finish.

13- Appearance of the finished piece.

Dark polychrome

One traditional way of polychroming pieces with colored finishes involved covering the object with gold leaf or even fine gold, and then coloring the piece with oils and letting the gold show through the transparency in certain places. These finishes, which could be somewhat loud, became more attractive with the passage of time. This patina that aged such pieces is the effect that's covered in the following paragraphs.

1- Prepare the piece by giving it a coat of acrylic primer-sealer and letting it dry for two hours. Paint the entire object evenly with yellow gold acrylic paint. Let it dry, and if necessary, give it a second coat so that it's even all over. Let dry 30 minutes.

2- Paint a part of the piece with a little medium green. This effect is easy to achieve if you apply the paint with your finger, rubbing gently and without totally covering the gold background color on the surface.

3- Use you finger to apply the rest of the chosen colors to the various details of the piece, without obscuring the base color or filling in the bas-relief. This is more like applying a little color that appears distressed.

4- If you want, you can also apply the color with a stenciling brush that's nearly dry; remove any excess with paper towels.

5- If the surface is too dark, you can remove some color by rubbing softly with a rag to let some of the base color show through. Let dry one hour.

6- Prepare a mixture of asphaltum and wax and use a bristle brush to spread it over the entire piece, being particularly careful in the corners and bas-relief.
The amount of patina to apply depends on the final effect you want to create; if you don't want a very dark finish, remove part of the patina with cotton rags.

- Before the patina dries, cover the whole piece with talc; the talc softens the high contrast and the darkness of the asphaltum and produces a softer finish. Let dry 24 hours. In some cases, you can use wood ash instead of talc to age the patina; the final result is darker and looks like the dust that some antique pieces have in their bas-relief. This option is often used in scenographic and special effects.

- Next, remove the excess talc with a dry sash brush, leaving a little bit in the bas-relief.

- Use a chamois cloth to buff the relief gently and unevenly and let some of the base colors show through. This allows you to soften the dark effect in some places and reveal the shades of the background.

0- Use your finger to apply some small bits of gilding wax to certain areas of relief to create some highlights; this produces a metallic shine similar to distressed gold. Let dry a half-hour. Use a chamois cloth or other soft cloth to shine the whole piece gently, taking particular care with the areas that were treated with the gilding wax.

11- Appearance of the finished piece.

Verdigris oxide

Using some common materials it's easy to create the metallic appearance, in a great variety of textures and colors, that's produced by some patinas, the passage of time, and the action of the elements. Many metal sculptors use processes that involve very toxic acids to create this effect on bronze, copper, and brass. But you can reproduce this finish on any type of surface if you use the color as a point of reference.

1- Prepare the plaster surface with a coat of primer sealer and let it dry for two hours. Paint the whole surface with dark green acrylic paint; if necessary, apply a second coat once it's dry. Let dry two hours.

2- Add a little oil of turpentine to some cobalt green oil paint to give it a creamy consistency; then apply it to the whole surface, varying the thickness and texture to give it a more realistic look and being particularly careful in the corners.

3- Use a soft cloth to buff the relief unevenly and remove the excess color in certain places.

4- Before the oil dries, moisten a sash brush in oil of turpentine and let it drip over the surface. The oil of turpentine makes some of the color run and produces a very convincing appearance of oxidation.

5- To accentuate the color contrast a little, use a rag moistened with turpentine to rub the surface and make some small spots distributed randomly that allow some of the base color to show through. Let dry 24 hours.

6- To create the highlights that metals have, use your finger to apply gilding wax unevenly to the parts of the relief that you want to stand out. Let dry a half-hour. Since there are various shades of gilding wax, the color can vary quite a bit, from reddish to more yellow, depending on the result you want to create.

7- Polish the whole piece with a chamois cloth or a soft cloth, being especially careful with the relief where you applied the metallic wax; this will produce a natural-looking shine.

8- Appearance of the finished piece.

Marble dust capital

The texture, color, and shape of a simple object give it an importance and a beauty with the passage of time. Architectural pieces and fragments that are recovered from excavation sites often have acquired a beauty that's attributable to the passage of time. Sometimes these effects are done to create atmosphere in decorating rooms and display windows; this may involve exceedingly distressed finishes that can make small pieces extremely decorative.

1- Apply a coat of acrylic primer-sealer to the whole piece and let dry two hours. Next, paint the entire piece with an even coat of dark brown acrylic paint. Let dry two hours.

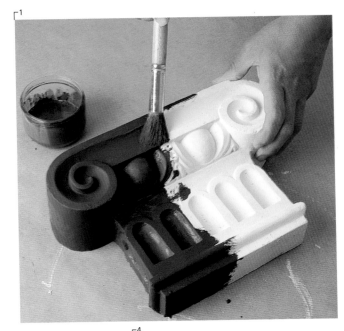

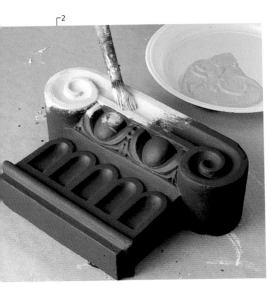

2- After the two hours have passed, apply some light beige, painting the entire piece by sections and unevenly.

3- Quickly, and before the paint dries, rub certain sections with a rag to let parts of the underlying color show through. Let dry a half-hour.
If the paint dries so much that you can't wipe it off, moisten a rag with a little alcohol and rub gently; be careful not to rub through the base color.

4- Darken certain areas of the piece with light brown paint; work in sections so that the paint doesn't get too dry.

5- Next, use a rag to rub here and there with varying pressure to mix the colors together. Let dry one hour. Superimposing different colors makes for a more convincing effect; it's important to work them in such a way that none of them totally covers the underlying color.

6- Dilute some matte oil-based varnish with oil of turpentine to create a solution of 70% varnish and 30% oil of turpentine. Varnish the whole piece with this solution, letting it accumulate unevenly in certain parts of the bas-relief. Let dry ten minutes until it becomes tacky.

7- Use a bristle brush to apply marble dust unevenly, filling up some relief areas; this will distress and eliminate some of the new shapes on the piece as the powder accumulates on them.

Different materials can be used to create this distressed effect; examples include sand or dirt of different grits and textures. Talc can also create this visual effect if used in greater quantities.

If you accidentally put on too much marble dust, you can remove it section by section, rubbing with a rag before the varnish starts to dry.

8- The marble dust is applied unevenly and more sparingly to flat surfaces by using your hands; it's best to apply just a little. Let the piece dry 24 hours.

9- Using a stiff scrub brush, remove any loose marble dust; scrub some areas lightly and others more forcefully.

10- To give the piece some color variety, shade certain areas very subtly with dark brown, applying the color with a nearly dry brush.

11- Use some light brown in the same way to create some lighter effects.

12- Appearance of the finished piece.

Bronze

Decorative painting is often used to make some objects appear to be made of some different material; by choosing the right colors, and with subtle patinas, some of these effects are truly impressive. Attempting to reproduce the appearance of certain metals can be fairly complicated. Imitating bronze by starting with pieces of plaster, plastic, or wood can be almost magical because the finish is visually so convincing. This torso of Mars is a good example.

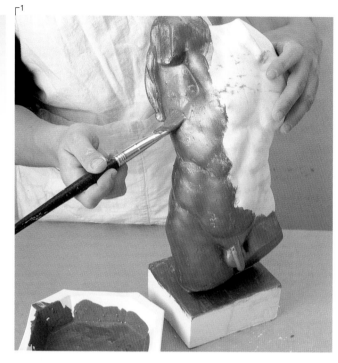

1- Prepare the piece with a coat of acrylic primer-sealer and let dry two hours. Apply a coat of bronze-colored acrylic paint to the entire piece and let dry two hours more. Metallic paints don't cover very well, and sometimes it's necessary to put on two or three coats to cover the surface thoroughly. Always let dry between coats.

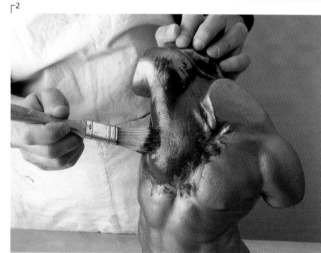

2- Apply the dark brown color section by section. Tap lightly with the brush; otherwise, the brush marks will spoil the effect.
Work in small areas, since acrylic paint dries very quickly.

3- Before the paint dries, remove some of the color by dabbing very gently with a rag; this lets some of the base color show through. Let dry one hour.

4- Apply the patina of asphaltum mixed with wax over the entire piece, being particularly careful in the bas-relief. Also gently dab this on with the brush.

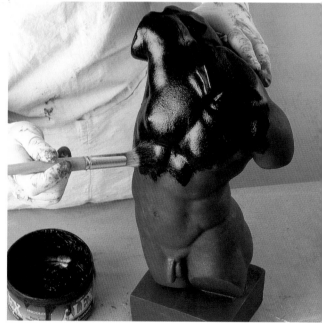

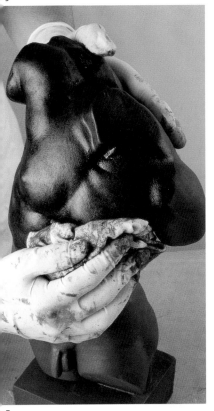

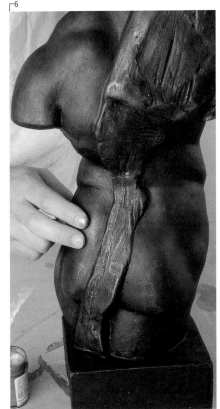

5- Press lightly with a rag to soften the dark effect, but don't wipe. Let the piece dry two hours.

6- Take a little bronze-colored wax on the tip of your finger and spread it out. Next, rub the high relief areas of the whole piece gently and unevenly without pressing too hard; let dry a half-hour.
Before applying the wax, see if the amount of wax is right by checking on a part of the piece that's not too visible; too much wax would create an exaggerated effect.
If the gilding wax creates an exaggerated effect in certain areas, rub some of it off by rubbing gently with clear wax; be careful you don't remove the asphaltum at the same time.

7- Buff the entire piece with a soft chamois cloth; this highlights the metallic effects produced by the gilding wax.

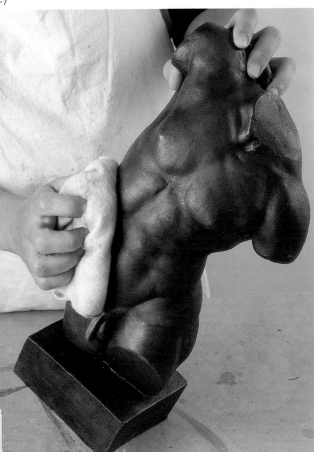

8- Appearance of the finished piece.

Old silver

Ever since the eighteenth century, painters have been imitating precious metals. Even though silver is not one of the most expensive ones, it too can be reproduced by means of painting. Nowadays there are pieces made of plaster, resin, and wood that look like authentic products from a silversmith. To make the appearance more convincing, it's important to choose the right type of object to decorate. A plaster frame is a fine candidate for this type of finish because of its elaborate ornamentation.

1- Apply a coat of acrylic primer-sealer to the entire piece and let it dry for two hours. Paint the whole object evenly with acrylic black paint. If necessary, apply a second coat once the first one is dry. Let dry one hour.

2- Paint the frame with silver acrylic paint without painting the bottom of the relief carving. Paint by sections so you can work before it dries.

3- Use a cotton cloth to rub the whole section unevenly in order to create different shades. Once you have finished painting and working the whole piece, let dry one hour.

4- Using a small brush, spread a coat of asphaltum mixed with wax onto the whole piece, paying particular attention to the corners.

5- Use a rag to remove part of the asphaltum before the mixture dries, producing an uneven appearance.

6- Sprinkle the whole piece with talc, and work it into the corners and the bas-relief with a small, stiff brush.

7- Next, use the same brush in gentle, circular motions to work the talc into the surface of the piece and make it stick.

8- Before it dries, rub gently with your hands so that the talc mixes and becomes integrated with the mixture of asphaltum and wax. Keep working it until the talc is dry and slips from your hands.

9- Use a dry brush to remove the talc and eliminate the excess left behind in the corners and the bas-relief.

10- Use a chamois cloth to get rid of the remaining talc by rubbing the whole piece. It's important to get rid of all the talc that is not stuck to the surface.

11- Take a small amount of silver wax on the tips of your fingers and gently rub the piece, emphasizing the raised carving. You can vary the darkness by applying more or less wax, continually rubbing gently. Let dry a half-hour and buff with a chamois cloth.

12- Appearance of the finished piece.

Staining and aging

Some familiar-looking antique or old furniture that formerly belonged to our ancestors may still be found in garages and attics; sometimes it has no value beyond the sentimental, and it may exhibit the dents and scratches that bear testimony to childhood mischief. The beauty that these pieces have taken on with the passage of time fills them with life and nostalgia. In the following exercise, you will learn how to reproduce the flavor of some of these objects by artificially speeding up the distress that old pieces exhibit.

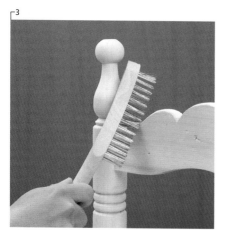

1- Put some screws and nails into a cotton rag to form a small bundle. It's best to use nails and bits of iron of different sizes for a variety of effects.

2- Next, strike some randomly chosen sections of the piece with varying force to produce a convincing effect and simulate small worm holes.

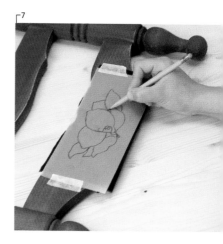

3- Use a wire brush to scratch the edges and distress them; this will make them look like they've been damaged over time. The scratches will vary in depth according to the force applied. Use a rag to get rid of any resulting dust.

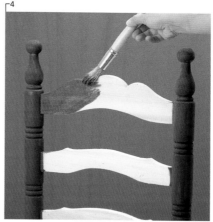

4- Prepare a transparent water-based glaze of medium brown color by mixing one part pigment to one part latex and four parts water. Stain the whole piece, following the wood grain as you brush on the glaze. Let dry two hours.

5- When you use a water-based stain, the surface of the wood may end up a little rough; if so, sand it lightly with medium-grit sandpaper so that it's smooth to the touch.

6- In order to protect the surface, apply a coat of matte oil-based varnish diluted to a solution of 70% varnish and 30% oil of turpentine; spread it out well so there are no drips or runs. Let dry 24 hours.

7- Trace the design selected for decorating the piece onto tracing paper and use a piece of carbon paper to trace it onto the back of the chair. Carbon paper may come in different colors; for dark surfaces, it's best to use light colors so that the design is easier to see.

8- Use artists' acrylic paints to color in the chosen design; use several light coats to produce greater depth, and gradually shade it and add some highlights to give the design some volume.

9- Choose a color that will stand out on the background to paint some details on the piece and make the decoration a little more elaborate. Let dry one hour.

10- Lightly sand the design with fine-grit sandpaper to create a slightly distressed effect. It wouldn't look right if the design looked as if it had just been painted. Remove any dust with a rag and varnish the parts decorated in color. Let dry 24 hours.

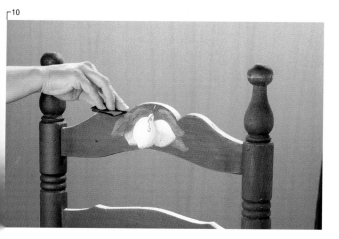

12- Appearance of the finished project.

11- Apply a coat of asphaltum and clear wax to the entire piece to darken it unevenly. Before it dries, remove the excess with a soft cotton cloth by dabbing gently and leaving the aged finish distributed unevenly. Let dry three hours and buff with a chamois cloth or a soft rag.

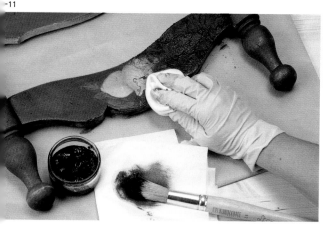

Golds and oxides

The process of gilding consists of applying gold, silver, or other metals in fine layers to certain surfaces.

To produce a good gilding, the base to which the layer of metal is applied must be as smooth as possible, since any defect or imperfection will show up in the final finish.

The various effects of oxidation that are described in the following paragraphs are done on layers of false gold; if real gold were used, it would not be possible to create the effects of oxidation with different acids.

You can get various chemical solutions to produce different oxidation effects, but some of them are very toxic or dangerous to handle. We have chosen products that are easy to find, some of which are probably already in your home, and that present no danger as you work to create the effects of oxidation.

Oxidized gum lacquer

Gum lacquer can't be considered a real oxidation, but the effect it creates in this exercise is very similar to what's found on some pieces that really are oxidized.

1- Usually when you prepare a surface for gilding, gesso is the primer of choice. In the present exercise, it's not essential that the surface be so smooth, since the idea is to produce an aged finish and create different effects afterwards.
Apply a uniform coat of acrylic primer-sealer to the whole piece and let it dry four hours.
If you want to produce a finish that has some texture, apply the primer using small brush strokes in all directions.

2- Choose the base color according to the contrast you want to create with the gold; in this case, a black oil-based satin-finish paint is applied to cover the entire surface thoroughly. Let dry eight hours.
The drying time for oil-based paint is indicated in the instructions of each manufacturer; as a result, drying time may vary. It's important to read the labels carefully on the products you use.

3- Dilute some oil varnish with oil of turpentine to a 50% solution; this will speed up drying time. Next, apply an even coat to the entire surface.
Let dry until it becomes tacky.

4- Next, gently press a gold leaf onto the surface, rubbing gently starting in one corner. Proceed in the same manner to attach the remaining leaves successively until the entire surface is covered.

5- Press the leaf gently with a cotton ball to eliminate bubbles and be sure that it sticks well to the entire surface. You can also use a soft-haired artist's smoothing brush to make the gold leaf adhere to the surface.
If there are any breaks or small uncovered areas, fill them up with small bits of metal leaf so that all the empty spots are covered.

6- Rub the surface gently with 000 steel wool to distress the metal leaf a little and let the base color show through for contrast.
If you want a more distressed appearance, moisten the pad of steel wool with a little oil of turpentine.

7- Tint gum lacquer with some burnt umber pigment to get a dark color. You can also use other pigments to color gum lacquer.
Paint the colored gum lacquer onto the gilded surface.

8- Quickly, before it starts to dry, use a slightly moistened brush to spatter the piece lightly with oil of turpentine. That will cause the gum lacquer to begin opening up in small spots, creating a very decorative oxidation effect. Let dry.
You can apply more coats using the same procedure, even changing the colors of the gum lacquer; let dry between coats.

Aging with oils

Traditionally, gold leaf has been decorated in thousands of different ways with oil paints. In this exercise, using a sponge and a contrasting shade of color, you can age the piece unevenly.

1- Apply a coat of dark green oil-based satin-finish paint to a surface previously prepared with acrylic primer-sealer. Let dry eight hours.

2- Cover the surface with layers of gold leaf as explained in the previous exercise.
Using 000 steel wool, gently rub the surface unevenly to create some more distressed areas.

3- Dilute some oil paint with a little oil of turpentine or essence of turpentine. Moisten a sponge in the paint and touch it gently in an irregular pattern to the gilded surface. Let dry 24 hours. To protect the piece, apply two coats of satin-finish polyurethane varnish, allowing adequate drying time between coats. You can vary the effect of the finish by applying different colors and alternating them to create different shades.

Oxidizing with potassium sulfite

The oxidation produced with potassium sulfite can be subtle or spectacular. It's important to test the concentration on some part of the piece to find out before-hand how it's going to react.

1- Apply a coat of oil-based satin-finish English red paint to a surface previously prepared with acrylic primer-sealer. You can choose other base colors to contrast with the oxidation.

2- Cover the surface of the piece with leaves of gilding metal. There are several different shades and types of metal laminates, ranging from copper to pewter and silver. Gently rub the gilded surface with 000 steel wool to distress it a little.

3- Dissolve the potassium sulfite, in an amount about the size of a chickpea, in ten scant tablespoons of water. The effect will vary according to the concentration of the mixture. Use protective gloves to handle the sulfite, since it's caustic and corrosive. Use a sponge moistened in the solution to apply the sulfite to the gilded surface in differing amounts. Set aside to dry so that the sulfite can begin to create the oxidation effects. The more concentrated the solution, the stronger its effect.

4- It's difficult to control the effect of oxidation, since finishes can turn out quite different depending on the ambient temperature and humidity. To stop the oxidation process and protect the piece, apply three coats of polyurethane varnish, allowing adequate drying time between coats.

Oxidizing with vinegar

The acid in vinegar produces a very attractive oxidation, depending on the amount of time it's allowed to work. Another household acid that will produce similar results is lemon juice. You can also use household bleach to produce very attractive effects on silver leaf.

1- Prepare the surface with acrylic primer-sealer. Choose a base color that contrasts with the gold leaf. In this case we are using a light bluish green oil-based satin-finish paint. Paint the surface of the object and let dry eight hours.

2- Apply metal leaf to cover the whole piece. Moisten pieces of paper towel in vinegar. You can get different types of vinegar that produce different results. In this case we are using common table vinegar.

3- Wrap the whole piece with moistened, wrinkled paper towel, leaving some sections uncovered. You have to press gently so that the paper sticks to the surface. The parts of the metal that come into contact with the paper are the ones that will oxidize and show the contrast with the base color. Let dry a few hours and check the process occasionally.

4- When you get the effect you want, carefully remove the pieces of paper towel from the whole piece. If you want a very pronounced effect, let it work up to 24 hours.

5- Once you obtain the desired degree of oxidation, rinse the surface with water to get rid of the vinegar and arrest the oxidation process. Apply three coats of polyurethane varnish, allowing sufficient drying time between coats.

6- Appearance of the finished project.

Glossary

Acrylic paint
Water-based paint that dries quickly; once dry, it's waterproof.

Agglutinating agents or binders
Substances of different origins whose function involves adhering and binding color pigments to a substrate.

Aging
Somewhat abrasive process used to simulate the passage of time or distress in wood, plastic, or new materials. Also a decorative process that lends an antique appearance to a painted surface by imitating dust.

Asphaltum
See Bitumen of Judea.

Bauhaus
German school of design from the 1920s; it introduced a new style that went beyond the differences between decorative art and engineering.

Base coat
The first layers of paint, whether alkyd or acrylic, that are applied as a base on which to create decorative effects.

Binder
See Agglutinating agents.

Bitumen of Judea or asphaltum
Black fossil resin used for aging effects. It's dissolved in oil of turpentine and is used mixed with clear beeswax to soften its effect.

Colorwashing
Attenuating a color so that it appears to melt or fade.

Combing
Effect produced by passing the tines of a rubber comb or a stiff brush over a surface moist with water or oil glaze.

Crackling
Appearance taken on by a surface whose paint has cracked. An effect caused by the passage of time and changes in temperature brought on artificially. Developed in France in the eighteenth century.

Crazing
See Crackling.

Decoupage
Style of decorating furniture, objects, and walls with paper cutouts, old illustrations, or photocopies.

Depth
Artistic process in which transparent paints or glazes are applied to create a cloudy effect, as if the viewer were penetrating to the background.

Double boiler
Vessel containing water that is applied to a source of heat; another container is placed inside the first so that its contents are subjected to a gentle and constant heat; very useful in preparing some glues and gesso.

Dragging
The effect produced by passing a moist, long-haired bristle brush over an oil or water glaze to create a series of fine lines on the surface being decorated.

Dryers
Chemical products that are added to mixtures of oil glazes to shorten drying time.

Dry brush
Painting process that consists of using a brush with very little paint to create a blurred effect, or to paint salient parts of an object.

Emulsion
More or less liquid, creamy texture of base paints

Essence of turpentine
A plant essence obtained by distilling the sap from certain conifers. Used as a diluting agent in oil paints. Is more pure than oil of turpentine.

Glacis (oil glaze)
Transparent mixture composed of turpentine, linseed oil, and dryer, plus a certain quantity of oil coloring or pigment.

Glaze
Very fluid and transparent paint used in superimposing one color on top of another after the first has dried in order to create various visual effects of depth. There are water, oil, and varnish glazes.

rain

⊃ paint the grain of marble in a special, ⊽isting pattern. Usually done with a fine ⊲ist's brush.

raining

⊾ethod used to imitate wood grain.

um lacquer

⊱esin produced by an insect, the lac beetle, the branches of the vegetation where it ⊽es. It's transparent and soluble in alcohol. ⊱ed similarly to varnishes for waterproofing ⊲fferent surfaces; also used to protect ⋂ishes such as gold leaf.

Highlight

touch created by different shades of paint create brighter and stronger values.

mitation

⋂nishes that simulate different materials ⊔ch as wood, stone, and marble. These ⊲fects are intentionally deceptive and are ⊱en referred to as faux finishes.

Kitsch

term used in reference to pieces or ⊵corations that look affected. Arose in mid-⋂eteenth century to distinguish between ⊷mething genuine and its imitation.

inseed oil

⊽egetable oil obtained from the flax plant; ⊱ed as a binder in preparing oil paints; also ⊵d for oil glazes

Marbling

⊲sual effect that mimics the appearance of ⋏arble

Mineral oil of turpentine

⊍btained form petroleum distillation, used as ⊲lvent for cleaning tools and brushes used ⊲ith oil techniques. Also used in preparing ⊾ glazes.

Monochrome

⋂ effect created with a single color and its ⊲fferent shades

Oil-based enamel

⊲il-based paint used for painting smooth surfaces or as a base for creating special effects in oils. Available in matte, satin, or gloss finishes.

Opaque

Opposite effect of transparent. Refers to paints with sufficient body to cover a surface totally, allowing none of the base paint to show through.

Patina

Color and texture that the surface of a material takes on due to erosion and the passage of time.

Polychrome

Effect created with various colors. Formerly used to refer to decorating baroque sculptures and images.

Primer-sealer

Emulsion similar to paints, used to prepare wood, plaster, and metal surfaces. Used so that paints and special effects applied to the surface adhere better and remain durable.

Rabbit-skin glue

Animal gelatin used as a glue and a binder; prepared using a double boiler.

Stenciling

Decorations on walls, furniture, or objects where templates are used to reproduce a painted design.

Tacky

Condition of paint, varnish, or glaze at the point that drying begins and the surface is sticky.

Tempera

Used in water-based techniques to bring a mixture or substance to the proper degree of adhesion and flexibility for good results. Normally used for egg tempera.

Texture

Process through which a finish takes on visual shape, or the tactile qualities of a material or a decorated surface.

Transparency

Visual effect produced by using water and oil glazes. Superimposing colors creates the appearance of depth.

Varnish

There are many types available on the market. Used to protect decorated surfaces. Available in oil, alcohol, and water bases. Each one is used for a specific purpose. Synthetic oil varnish is used in preparing oil glazes.

Vegetable oil of turpentine

Obtained by distilling the resins of certain conifers. The most highly esteemed type comes from the cluster or maritime pine. More refined than turpentine, it is used as a solvent and in the preparation of oil glazes.

Wainscoting

Lower part of a wall that is painted or papered. Functions to protect against dents and scratches, as well as to add decoration.

Wash

Diluted water-based paint used to create a transparent finish. Formerly produced by adding pigment to whitewash.

Wear and tear

Process of distressing an object or a new surface to make it look old.

ACKNOWLEDGMENTS

To Jordi and my children for their tremendous patience and support. Also to Adriana Berón for her great help and confidence. To Ramon Peñarroya, who has always supported me and made available to me everything I have needed. To my friends Antonio, who is always available and willing to help, and Pedro García for his great help and constant good cheer.

DECORATIVE PAINTING

Original title of Spanish book:
Pintura Decorativa

© Copyright 1999 by Parramon Ediciones, S.A.
World Rights
Gran Via de les Corts Catalanes, 322–324
08004 Barcelona, Spain

Text and Exercises:
Maria Victoria López Santacruz

Translated from the Spanish by:
Eric A. Bye, M.A.

Photography:
Nos & Soto, Boreal, Vnu Tijdschriften

English edition for the United States, Canada, and its territories and possessions © copyright 2000 by Barron's Educational Series, Inc.

All inquiries should be addressed to:
Barron's Educational Series, Inc.
250 Wireless Boulevard
Hauppauge, New York 11788
http://www.barronseduc.com

International Standard Book No. 0-7641-1550-

Library of Congress Catalog Card No. 99-68838

PRINTED IN SPAIN

9 8 7 6 5 4 3 2 1